OSTIUM AB INFERNO
[The Opening From Hell]

OSTIUM AB INFERNO

[The Opening From Hell]

The Original Monograph—According to The Father, The Christ Son, and The Holy Ghost

Danté Camminatore

Quadrakoff Publications Group, LLC
Wilmington, Delaware
USA

Copyright © 2020, 2019 Quadrakoff Publications Group, LLC All rights reserved.

Except as noted, All Scripture passages taken from The Holy Bible, King James Version.
All NASB scriptures taken from The New American Standard Bible® Copyright © 1960, 1962, 1963, 1968, 1971, 1972, 1973, 1975, 1977, 1995 by the Lockman Foundation, LaHabra, CA.

Special thanks to the Lockman Foundation for the finest Bible version available; as well as for their permission to use the same.

ISBN: 978-1-948219-66-2

All rights reserved. No part of this publication may be reproduced, stored in a retrieval system or transmitted, in any form, or by any means, electronic, mechanical, recorded, photocopied, or otherwise, without the prior written permission of both the copyright owner and the above publisher of this book, except by a reviewer who may quote brief passages in a review.

The scanning, uploading, and distribution of this book via the Internet or via any other means without the permission of the publisher is illegal and punishable by law. Please purchase only authorized electronic editions and do not participate in or encourage electronic piracy of copyrightable materials. Your support of the author's rights is appreciated.

Printed in the United States of America.

Any and all characters appearing that are not in any of the versions of the Bible are fictional. Any resemblance to any living person is strictly coincidental.

Contents

Foreword -- xi

Le Stipulazioni
[The Stipulations] --- 1

L'inizio del Tempo
[The Beginning of Time] --- 3

Causando un Posto per Loro
[Causing a Place for Them] --- 7

Lazzaro, L'uomo Ricco, e il Seno
[Lazarus, the Rich Man, and the Bosom] ----------------------------- 19

Comunicare con Quelli nel Seno
[Communicating With Those in the Bosom] ----------------------- 29

La Fisica Dell'attività Demoniaca
[The Physics of Demonic Activity] ------------------------------------ 35

L'enigma
[The Conundrum] --- 43

Le Cose Erano Diverso Modo Indietro Allora
[Things Were Different Way Back Then] --------------------------- 59

Angeli per Struttura
[Angels by Structure] --- 65

Ciò Che è Noto—Una Ricapitolazione
[That Which is Known—A Recapitulation] ------------------------- 83

Demoni nella Bibbia
[Demons in the Bible] -- 87

Le Aperture Che Contano per L'uomo
[The Openings That Matter to Man] -------------------------------- 103

About the MeekRaker Title --- 121

Bibliography --- 125

Non sai di cosa sono capaci.
[*You do not know what they are capable of.*]

FOREWORD

È *Da* o *Verso* Che Dovrebbe Essere di Maggiore Preoccupazione?

[Is *To* or *From* That Should Be of Greater Concern?]

Much is often said about the roads, doors, or gates *to* hell. Whether being paved with "good intentions," or the result of non-upright behavior, (sin or *senza*); the overwhelming preoccupation is with the means of arriving at this destination. These are how one enters *into* hell; and generally the main interest is the avoidance of ever traveling through this or these openings, and arriving at this destination.

The truth is; that that which caused all that exists *to* exist; i.e.; the *primum-movens*, or first mover (*primo motore*), the "*effect* with no *cause*;" is perfect. And that perfection cannot permit *any* contamination by that which is imperfect. And since all men sin, it necessarily follows that no man can be permitted to reattach to that which is perfect, and no amount of good works can ever undo this.

Salvation by justification is the only way to avoid this separation; whether salvation be available now, as per Christian beliefs; or will be available sometime in the future, as per the other two

"Abrahamic" religions: Judaism and Islam. This is the *only* way one can prevent traversing this opening to hell. Thus it seems that little attention should be paid to the opening *into* hell, as nothing short of accepting salvation can ever change this.

But the opening *from* hell is another matter. There are entities; including many non- human entities; currently "residing" in hell, and they do not wish to remain there. And for the very same reasons these entities were sent there, they remain a danger to man.

What is hell? Why is there a hell? What openings from "hell" are there? And how does this or do these affect man? Much of that which is fanciful has been written about these questions. But the answers should not be sought from that which is the product of men's imaginations—albeit these may provide interesting reading. Rather; the answers should be sought from, and always remain: "according to The Father, The Christ Son, and The Holy Ghost."

—*Danté Camminatore*

Le Stipulazioni

[The Stipulations]

What do we genuinely know? Ask any true solipsist (not sophist) this question, and the likely response will be: "I only genuinely *know* that I (the solipsist) exist—all else may be mere speculation."

And there is some truth in this response—if "genuinely know" is the test. But if that is the test, it seems that there would be no point in much of anything, except perhaps survival. Thus certain stipulations must be made regarding what exists and what does not exist.

That which truly *exists* is an *actuality*. That which is *perceived* to exist is *reality*. A mirage has the *reality* of water, but the *actuality* of anything except water—if it is a mirage. *Realization* is the process by which an actuality is perceived. *Actualization* is the process whereby that which is or was "perceived;" such as that which is in ones imagination; is brought into existence as an actuality.

That which exists, exists irrespective of the existence of any reality regarding the same. That which does not exist, does not exist, irrespective of the existence of any reality regarding the same—unless and until it is ultimately actualized.

Doxa can be roughly defined as "probable truth." *Episteme* can be roughly defined as "certain truth." But of course to the aforementioned solipsist; his existence is the only "certain" truth. Thus to the same extent that this may be true, there is likewise little or no choice other than that any other *episteme* or "certain truth," must be determined by some level of proof less than certainty. Oxymoronic as this may seem, there is little choice.

So again there must be at least the following fundamental stipulations:

- The first stipulation is that something other than ourselves exists.
- A thing that is, is; and thus cannot simultaneously not be.
- In the long term Science; meaning "to know;" is ultimately generally correct most of the time—Max Planck's quote about "Science changes one funeral at a time." notwithstanding. Ultimately, they "get it right."
- The Bible; if correctly understood; must be consistent with science, else at least one is incorrect.
- Every effect must have a cause; every cause has an effect.

> "Logic alone will not tell you what you do not know, for that you need rhēma or lŏgŏs. But logic can show you that which you know, but did not know you knew."
> —Emma B. Quadrakoff

L'inizio del Tempo

[The Beginning of Time]

Genesis 1:1 (KJV) tells us:

> *"In the beginning God created the heaven(s) and the earth."*[1]

The event described in this passage is often referred to as the "Big Bang" in scientific, or at least *quasi*-scientific communities. If one watched the events described in Genesis 1:1, one would have witnessed this Big Bang. But because of the common knowledge (*doxa*) regarding other events described in the Bible, there is disagreement regarding *when* this happened.

This disagreement begins largely because of the conflating of the *creation* (H. *bârâ'*) of original mankind from *nothing material* hundreds of thousands of years ago; with the *formation* (H. *yâtsar*) of Adam from *something* material (H. *'âphâr*) less than ten thousand years ago. And then adamantly (no pun intended), believing and maintaining these separate and mutually exclusive (either matter was utilized or it was not) events to be the *same* event.

It then "logically" follows that since the formation of Adam is reasonably known to have occurred less than ten thousand years ago, that this then must likewise necessarily also be the age of the earth. This is then further compounded by assuming that a "day" (H. *yom*) necessarily means *kronos* or a literal chronological day, despite the lack of luminaries early on; rather than considering the equally acceptable definition of a *period of activity* or *chiros*. [See "MeekRaker Beginnings..." Ch. 1-4]

But whether it is Genesis 1:1 or it is the "Big Bang" that is utilized; we are told much more than is actually stated by either:

No rational mind would argue that the creation of the material universe does not represent an effect. Biblically the cause of this effect is stated. It is unclear whether science has yet established a plausible cause for this effect; but both Biblically and scientifically some type of *cause* is both acknowledged and required for this *effect* known as the universe.

At some point there was no material universe, and at some point there then was—and the Bible and science agree on this fact. Thus the *cause* for the effect known as the material universe had to exist *prior* to the event of the creation of the same. Irrespective if it was God as the Bible states; or some other proffered cause; the same question remains: Whence, or from *where* came this cause?

It can be stated with 100% certainty that this cause could not have emanated from a realm that did not yet exist; i.e.; the cause for the existence of the material universe could not have existed in that universe which was yet to exist. Thus it must have emanated from a realm other than the material universe.

What is or was it that was created in Genesis 1:1, AKA: "The Big Bang," irrespective of any given purported cause? The answer is matter, space, and time. It then logically follows that this required "other realm" has or had no matter, no space, and no time. Perhaps there is another material universe from which this cause emanated, but no evidence exists in support of this, and this dilemma would likely merely repeat itself *ad-infinitum* and *ad-nauseam*. This position would be further complicated by the fact that both Genesis

1:1 and arguably science agree that *no* matter was utilized in the bringing forth the material universe.

This quasi-eponymous immaterial realm is often referred to as "heaven;" but never "the heavens." "The heavens" is the "space" between the celestial bodies— essentially a "matter-less" part of the *material* universe. Heaven is the *immaterial* realm where God "art in." There is neither matter, nor space, nor time in this immaterial realm or "heaven."

At some point after the creation of the universe, man entered the scene. Although there is little detailed information about the actual *process* by which the original hosts were *created*; we are told Biblically how it was that Adam was brought into existence via the *formation* of existing matter at a much later time:

Genesis 2:7 (KJV) tells us:

> "And the LORD God formed man of the dust of the ground, and breathed into his nostrils the breath of life; and man became a living soul."[2]

The bringing forth of the existence of (non-created) man here in Genesis 2:7 is a two-part process. And likewise *scientifically* speaking; first the vessel is formed, and then this immaterial part is introduced. There are two significant differences between how this is done today, and how Adam came into existence:

Again "scientifically" speaking; today the vessel is formed, in and by, another human vessel (gestation); as opposed to God Himself forming Adam's vessel. Another difference is that much of science believes that only matter (air) enters the vessel with the first breath; rather than air, along with the immaterial "breath of life."

Physical "life" or "alive" is considered that union of the physical body with that immaterial part of man or soul. Before the first breath there is no physical life. After the last breath there is no longer physical life. Physical life is that period of time in between these two respective breaths.

After the last breath, that immaterial part leaves the body and "goes somewhere." The physical body "remains," and is subject to physical laws.

But where does that immaterial portion "normally" go?

This is where science currently has no answer, but the Bible does. If the immaterial portion of man were never contaminated by sin, it simply returns to the immaterial realm, to its source. If it was contaminated by sin, then a "reverse quarantine" exists. No contaminated soul can be permitted to re-enter the immaterial realm and reconnect to its source, lest the entire immaterial realm then become likewise contaminated.

Without getting into too much religious doctrine, this is the reason man needs salvation. Since all men sin (except one), no man's immaterial part or soul can return to the immaterial realm and its source, without salvation via justification. A contaminated soul in the absence of salvation goes to a place often referred to as hell.

Spiritual life or "alive," is the condition where this immaterial portion of man is either connected or *re-connected* to the immaterial realm source; i.e.; in *heaven*.

Spiritual death or "dead" is where this immaterial portion is *disconnected* from the material realm source; i.e.; "in hell."

Causando un Posto per Loro

[Causing a Place for Them]

Revelation 12:7-9 (KJV) tells us:

*"And there was war in heaven:
Michael and his angels fought
against the dragon; and the dragon
fought and his angels,
And prevailed not; neither was
their place found any more in heaven.
And the great dragon was cast out,
that old serpent, called the Devil, and Satan,
which deceiveth the whole world:
he was cast out into the earth, and
his angels were cast out with him."*[3]

Here we have a description of what happened; (most likely at some point in time between Genesis 1:1 and Genesis 1:2); when sin attempted to contaminate the immaterial realm or heaven. Although very little is known regarding the circumstances surrounding this battle, what is clear is that there was then no place "any more" for the enemy or "his angels" in the immaterial realm or "heaven," and they were "cast out."

The actual Greek word translated as "angels" is:

>32 "aggĕlŏs; from aggĕllō; (prob. der. from 71; comp. 34) (to *bring tidings*); a *messenger*; esp. an *"angel"*; by impl. a *pastor*:- angel, messenger."[4]

The word aggĕlŏs is the only word used for "angels" in the entire New Testament except in Luke 20:36 which is:

>"2465 siaggĕlŏs; from 2470 and 32; *like an angel*, i.e. *angelic*: - equal unto the angels."[5]

Just for reference, Luke 20:36 (KJV) tells us:

>*"Neither can they die any more: for they are equal unto the angels; and are the children of God, being the children of the resurrection."*[6]

The definition of the aggĕlŏs requires three things. First; one who sends a message or tidings. Second; the message or tidings itself or themselves. And third; a recipient for the message or tidings. The significance of this will be addressed later.

It must be noted that the actual Greek word translated as "deceiveth" is:

"4105 planaō; from *4106*; to (prop. *cause to*) *roam* (from safety, truth, or virtue): - go astray, deceive, err, seduce, wander, be out of the way."[7]

Thus here there are actually two matters to consider. The *objective of* these particular aggĕlŏs, is or was planaō; or "to (prop. *cause to*) *roam* (from safety, truth, or virtue): - go astray, deceive, err, seduce, wander, be out of the way." The "these," in this context, is important because not all angels or aggĕlŏs seek planaō. It was only *these particular* angels or aggĕlŏs; those "cast out with him; who sought and seek planaō. Those who were not "cast out;" i.e.; are not with the enemy, are likewise aggĕlŏs; but they do not seek planaō.

As an aside, it is considered "common knowledge" or *doxa* that the enemy took *one third* of the angels with him; however there seems to be little Biblical evidence for this.

Revelation 12:4 is usually cited as the source for this "took one third" belief:

Revelation 12:4 (KJV) tells us:

> "And his tail drew the third part of the stars of heaven,
> and did cast them to the earth:
> and the dragon stood before the woman
> which was ready to be delivered,
> for to devour her child as soon as it was born."[8]

There are several problems with citing this verse as evidence for the "one third" theory: Revelation 12:9 tells us the enemy: "*was cast out into the earth, and his angels were cast out with him.*" Thus it was not the enemy who did any casting out of these *aggĕlŏs*; whether by utilizing his tail, or by any other means—they were "thrown out" together.

Neither Satan nor these aggĕlŏs were active parties in this expulsion event; i.e.; they were the "baseballs" and not the "batter." And given the context, the timing is way off, unless one believes that *"the woman which was ready to be delivered, for to devour her child as soon as it was born;"* had already occurred long long ago. And also given the context, it seems that this "tail action" relates to an entirely different event, and an event in the far future.

There are both similarities and differences with respect to the enemy and a contaminated soul:

The enemy was *cast out* of the immaterial realm; (*heaven* but not the heavens); because of the contamination of sin committed while in that realm. The actual word here in this passage of Revelation translated as "into" is:

> "*1519* ĕis *to* or *into* (indicating the point reached or entered) of place, time, or (fig) purpose (result etc.)"⁹

So at this point it is unclear whether "to the earth" or "into the earth" represents the correct translation.

Man is refused *reentry*, because of sin committed while in the condition of physical life.

Although the actual genesis of the enemy is not known, it seems clear that the enemy is an immaterial entity, and was designed to exist, and did in fact exist, in the immaterial realm; and thus was not designed to exist in the material realm. We are told that he was cast out of the immaterial realm, either *to* the earth or *into* the earth. But as a *material* entity on the *material* realm, the enemy is not generally recognizable as such.

At the risk of a "double tautology," it must again be stated that the immaterial part of man is immaterial in nature, and the material part of man is material. The true part or essence of man (the part that is created equal), is the immaterial part; with the material part representing a vessel for earthly (material) existence. The immaterial part is immortal, but the physical part, under normal circumstances, is not—at least by the "normal" rules of the material realm.

For clarity, distinctions must be made. It is beyond any rational dispute, that there is an immaterial realm with "current lawful occupants." God and angels (*non-planaō* seeking angels) come to mind first. To the extent that there are other *immaterial* entities that exist, these either "lawfully reside" in the immaterial realm as per design, or they do not. To be clear, this: "do not" does not mean *unlawful* residence in the immaterial realm, as we are told what happens when this is attempted. This refers to immaterial entities that may in fact exist, but do not exist or "reside" in the immaterial realm. There may be a plethora of other entities legitimately residing in the immaterial realm, or there may not be. However the enemy and "his angels" although they continue to exist, we are told they no longer reside in the immaterial realm as they by design should—and by design they do not possess an earthly vessel, and thus cannot have any type of "normal material" existence.

The material and immaterial realms are a binary; in that there is either matter or there is not. Any entity who either cannot re-enter the immaterial realm (contaminated soul); or one who was "cast out" of the immaterial realm, cannot exist in or on that realm. And if *neither* has the physical vessel to exist in the material realm; e.g.; an entity originally designed for immaterial existence, or a soul departed from said physical vessel (no longer has an "earth suit"); then neither can either of the same truly exist in the material realm.

The "nether world" is generally considered to be that which is down or beneath the surface of the earth; arguably the "bad section" of the *immaterial* realm; with perhaps the surface of the earth being the "tracks" which this nether world is on the "bad side" of. This would be consistent with the "cast out *into* the earth" translation of the aforementioned *ĕis*.

Merriam Webster defines "nether" as:

> "1: situated down or below: lower; 2: situated or believed to be situated beneath the earth's surface."[10]

But although this "nether world" may not be material, "neither" is it necessarily any part of the immaterial realm.

It could in fact be; any "etymological sources" to the contrary not withstanding; that this "nether" merely represents a misspelling of "neither."

11

If so, this would represent both a kind of third realm; and *not* a third realm simultaneously. Meaning; that the *"neither world;"* as opposed to the common usage of *"nether* world;" actually means *neither* realm or "world;" or "stuck" between the two realms. This would be an "X realm;" and is not *either* realm; but rather *neither* realm, or *no realm.*

This may have been the actual source of the now abandoned concept of "Limbo." The Catholic doctrine of Limbo was concerned with that place where those who were not "Baptized;" usually infants; supposedly went upon physical death. The belief is or was; that *all* (except Jesus) are born with "original sin," which is removed only with Baptism. Since the belief is that no one can go to heaven unless cleansed of this and all other sins; there then had to be a place for infants who are all born with original sin; but yet could not have sinned of their own free will. No attempt is being made here to attest to the truth or falsity of any particular religious beliefs, including this one; but merely to present them.

Thus this concept of "Limbo" represented a destination between heaven and hell. According to this doctrine, the infant *could* not go to heaven because of the original sin; yet *should* not go to hell because infants do not know right from wrong, and thus cannot sin of their own free will. Hence there had to be a benign place that was in the immaterial realm, but technically not part of "heaven."

However; it is possible that originally this concept of "Limbo" referred to not a section of the *immaterial* realm outside of heaven, but rather to be caught *in between* the material and immaterial realms—this *neither* world, AKA: the "X" or the "no realm."

The word "limbo" can refer to either a dance which was popular in the 1950's and/or the 1960's; or it refers to something else. That something else can be seen from the root of the word.

Limbo is derived from:

> "Latin (in) *limbō* (on) the edge, ablative case of *limbus* edge, border..."[11]

Limbo originally likely meant this border or edge between the two realms; rather than a separate place within a realm; here a separate "place" as or like the immaterial realm; in terms of including no space, time, or matter; but not actually within either realm. This can also be seen with the common usage of "stuck in limbo;" which means stuck between two things, and unable to move forward or backward.

The common concept (doxa) of "hell" requires a bit of analysis. It is generally considered as a possible destination for the immaterial portion of life forms—those with the "breath of life." However the origin of the word "hell" seems a bit sketchy.

According to Etymonline.com, "hell" is from:

> "Old English hel, helle, "nether world, abode of the dead, infernal regions, place of torment for the wicked after death," from Proto-Germanic *haljō "the underworld" (source also of Old Frisian helle, Old Saxon hellia, Dutch hel, Old Norse hel, German Hölle, Gothic halja "hell").
>
> "Literally "concealed place" (compare Old Norse hellir "cave, cavern"), from PIE root *kel-(1) "to cover, conceal, save." The English word may be in part from Old Norse mythological Hel (from Proto-Germanic *halija "one who covers up or hides something"), in Norse mythology the name of Loki's daughter who rules over the evil dead in Niflheim, the lowest of all worlds (nifl "mist"). A pagan concept and word fitted to a Christian idiom.
>
> "In Middle English, also of the Limbus Patrum, place where the Patriarchs, Prophets, etc. awaited the Atonement."[12]

It should be noted here that the etymology of "atone," is actually the fusion of the words "at" and "one." Here we have the use of Limbus Patrum, or the limbo of the fathers in the description and etymology of hell? What is this Limbus Patrum? This is the "place" where the immaterial part of those "Patriarchs, Prophets, etc.;" i.e.;

13

those great men of the Bible; "went" because salvation was unavailable to them while they were physically alive. Arguably this is a *temporary* condition, unlike the purported concept of limbo for un-baptized children. So if you lived *before* Jesus provided salvation; and having committed all types of sins, you were sent to a *temporary* limbo. But with this "original sin and Limbo" theory, if you were born after salvation was available, and having been incapable of sinning, but remained uncleansed of original sin; this limbo was *permanent*.

It seems that the original meaning of hell had much more to do with a "concealed place" or "to cover, conceal;" rather than a fiery place where some souls go for eternal punishment. It must be asked as to precisely from what it is that this "place" known as hell provides concealment? It could metaphorically be asked if twilight conceals the dark from the light; or if twilight conceals the light from the dark.

The use of the term infernal:

> "*adj.* about 1385 *infernal* of hell, in Chaucer's *Canterbury Tales*; borrowed from Old French *infernal*, from Late Latin *īnfernālis* belonging to the lower regions, from *īnfernus* hell, literally, the lower world, noun use of Latin *īnfernus* situated below, of the lower regions, lower, related to *īnfernus* below; see UNDER."[13]

Likely the idea of inferno representing a hot or fiery area, was the result of the conflating of the hot "lower regions," or what is "UNDER" the material earth, with this immaterial-like "place;" that is neither within the immaterial realm or heaven; nor is it a part of the material realm.

"Into the earth" in the literal *material* sense, means substantial increases in temperature; i.e.; as calculable per the *geothermal gradient*. But since heat as we know it is the movement of material phenomena, it seems difficult to conceive of heat in any realm or world without matter.

As previously stated, there are two types of "death." There is *physical* death: where the soul et al. is no longer "contained" in the body. There is also so called *spiritual* death: where after physical death, this soul cannot be (re)connected to or in the presence of God because of sin. Cemeteries, mausoleums and the like; are generally not considered as in any way synonymous with hell. Thus, the above definition of hell as "abode of the dead" cannot in any way refer to the abode of the *material* portion of man. Ergo, it is only the *immaterial* portion of man which can abide in hell. But the immaterial portion of man is immortal; else how could there be eternal punishment in hell; or eternal happiness in heaven? It can and should be fairly asked how it could be that this immaterial portion of man could actually die? The answer is that it does not. This "death" is spiritual death, and refers to the immaterial portion not being connected to or in the presence of God after physical death.

If it is stipulated that this nether (neither) world is as it appears to be, then whether called nether world, hell or limbo; it represents a "place" "where" immaterial entities reside that is in between the two (material and immaterial) realms. That which is in this neither or nether world; is concealed from both the material and the immaterial realms.

Thus at least conceptually, there must be at least two "edges" or "borders" ["Latin (in) limbō (on) the edge, ablative case of limbus edge, border..."] providing this area of "concealment." One "edge" or "border" conceals this area from the immaterial realm, and prevents entrance to the same. And the other conceals this area from the material realm, and prevents entrance into the same.

The desired result by design, is that any entity present "there," is "stuck" in between the two realms and cannot of his own choosing move into either the material or the immaterial realm. But just as the "fine print" is provided to prove that whatever is boldly stated in the "large print" is patently false; here there is also a "catch."

> *"That which is stated in the "fine print," provides the explanation as to why that which is stated in the "large print" is false—else "fine print" would be unnecessary."*—Emma B. Quadrakoff

Genesis 1:26-28 (KJV) tells us:

> "And God said, Let us make man in our image,
> after our likeness: and let them have dominion
> over the fish of the sea, and over the fowl of the air,
> and over the cattle, and over all the earth, and over
> every creeping thing that creepeth upon the earth.
> So God created man in his own image,
> in the image of God created he him;
> male and female created he them.
> And God blessed them, and God said unto them,
> Be fruitful, and multiply, and replenish the earth,
> and subdue it: and have dominion
> over the fish of the sea, and over the fowl
> of the air, and over every living
> thing that moveth upon the earth"[14]

The actual word translated here as "earth" is:

> "776 'erets; from an unused root prob. mean to *be firm*; the *earth* (at large, or partitively a *land*): - common, country, earth, field, ground, land, x nations, way, + wilderness, world."[15]

It seems that translating *'erets* as "earth," may be a bit of an understatement. Given that "be firm" seems to be the better translation of *'erets*; this likely means the *entire* material realm or all that is "firm;" as opposed to that which is *spiritus* (spirit) or breathlike; as in the *immaterial* realm or *heaven* (but not the *heavens*). This could then include all that is "firm" in the entire material universe, and not merely "earth."

And the actual word utilized as "subdue" is the Hebrew:

> "3533 kâbash; a prim root; to *tread* down; hence neg. to *disregard*; pos. to *conquer, subjugate, violate*."[16]

And it must be noted that "bring into bondage," is another translation of kâbash.[7] It is from kâbash, that the English word *kibosh* is derived. So man is actually literally instructed by God to "put the kibosh" (sometimes *kybosh*) on the earth, and/or all that is "firm."

Just as an aside, an English word with the root "firm," is seen in the translations of early Genesis. Whenever the word translated as "firmament" appears in the Old Testament, it is:

> "7549 râqîya'; from 7554; prop. an *expanse*, i.e. the *firmament* or (apparently) visible arch of the sky:- firmament"[8]

> "7554 râqa'; a prim. root; to *pound* the earth (as a sign of passion); by analogy to *expand* (by hammering); by impl. to *overlay* (with thin sheets o metal): - beat, make broad, spread abroad (forth, over, out, into plates), stamp, stretch."[9]

And just for reference, Genesis 1:6-8 (KJV) tells us:

> "And God said, Let there be a firmament
> in the midst of the waters,
> and let it divide the waters from the waters.

> "And God made the firmament, and
> Divided the waters which were under
> the firmament from the waters which were
> above the firmament: and it was so.

> "And God called the firmament Heaven.
> And the evening and the morning
> were the second day."[20]

As previously stated, and unlike the "edge" or "border" as provided by a door into a room from a hallway; "there must be *two* "edges" or "borders" providing "doors" to this (neither or nether world or hell) area.

One conceals this area (nether world or hell) from the *immaterial* realm and prevents entrance to the immaterial realm. And the other conceals this area from the *material* realm and prevents entrance into the same. One border or barrier is likely immaterial, and under God's control. Whether the other is material, immaterial, or "both" cannot reasonably be deduced.

The *former* (immaterial) edge, or border must exist—else how was it that Satan and his aggĕlŏs were placed in there to begin with? As previously stated, this particular event may have in fact established the area. In addition, it must continue to exist as an entrance for contaminated souls, whether or not it was an entrance (and ultimate exit for some), for those in the "Limbus Patrum."

And the *latter* (material) edge, or border must also exist—else how was it that the enemy (as *nâchâsh* or hisser) managed to get to Adam & Co. in the *material gan* or guarded area (often translated as garden) in Eden; to Jesus after His fasting; to Jesus in Gethsemane, as well as the enemy's other material "appearances?"

But unlike the immaterial or *spiritus* realm barrier; (leading into the "non-'erets" or *immaterial* realm, or "heaven"); over which man does *not* have jurisdiction or control; man likely has jurisdiction and control over that barrier *into the material world*, no matter what its composition—and irrespective of whether man is aware of this at any given time or not. However strange all of this may sound, this nevertheless does best explain the maximum number of "knowns."

One need not be a philosophunculist to say: "Wait a minute the Bible says…;" and then cite Luke 16:19-31 as clearly contradicting the permeability of these "two barriers."

Lazzaro, L'uomo Ricco, e il Seno

[Lazarus, the Rich Man, and the Bosom]

Luke 16:19-31 (KJV) tells us:

*"There was a certain rich man,
which was clothed in purple and fine linen,
and fared sumptuously every day:*

*"And there was a certain beggar named Lazarus,
which was laid at his gate, full of sores,
And desiring to be fed with the crumbs which
fell from the rich man's table: moreover the dogs
came and licked his sores.*

*"And it came to pass,
that the beggar died, and was carried by the angels into
Abraham's bosom: the rich man also died,
and was buried;*

"And in hell he lift up his eyes,
being in torments, and seeth Abraham afar off,
and Lazarus in his bosom.

"And he cried and said, Father Abraham,
have mercy on me, and send Lazarus, that he may
dip the tip of his finger in water, and cool my tongue;
for I am tormented in this flame.

"But Abraham said, Son, remember that thou
in thy lifetime receivedst thy good things,
and likewise Lazarus evil things:
but now he is comforted, and thou art tormented.

"And beside all this, between us and you
there is a great gulf fixed: so that they which
would pass from hence to you cannot;
neither can they pass to us,
that would come from thence.

"Then he said, I pray thee therefore, father,
that thou wouldest send him to my father's house:
For I have five brethren; that he may testify unto them,
lest they also come into this place of torment.

"Abraham saith unto him, They have Moses
and the prophets; let them hear them.
And he said, Nay, father Abraham:
but if one went unto them from the dead,
they will repent. And he said unto him,
If they hear not Moses and the prophets,
neither will they be persuaded,
though one rose from the dead."[21]

So we have two individuals here: one is an unnamed rich man, hereafter known as "RM;" and the other one is a beggar named Lazarus. Generally "parables" do not include actual names, and thus do not represent recollections of actual events. "Stories" generally do include actual names, and thus do represent recollections of actual events.

Here we have a beggar named Lazarus, and a "rich man" whose name is not provided. Thus it is not clear if this is a recollection of actual events, or a parable utilized for teaching.

The actual Greek word translated here as "Lazarus," is a bit difficult to ascertain. Strong indicates that "Lazarus" in this passage is:

> "2976 Lazarŏs; prob. of Heb. or. [499]; *Lazarus* (i.e. *Elazar*), the name of two Isr. (one imaginary): - Lazarus."[22]

It remains unclear if the Lazarus in these passages is the "imaginary" Israelite, or if a translation problem exists. As it reads, Lazarus shows up at RM's gate; *"full of sores"* and desiring food. It seems that Lazarus must have been *brought* to RM's gate, as we are told he was *"laid at his gate."* We are not told who it was that may have brought Lazarus to RM's gate, and then "laid" Lazarus there.

We are not told here what else happened with Lazarus when he was alive, other than the *"dogs came and licked his sores."* We are not told if RM fed or housed Lazarus, as the next thing we are told is that they both died. Lazarus was then *"carried by the angels into Abraham's bosom;"* and RM *"was buried; and in hell he lift up his eyes, being in torments, and seeth Abraham afar off, and Lazarus in his bosom."*

So here we first have angels carrying Lazarus to Abraham's Bosom. [It is unclear as to how this action represents any type of *message* or *tidings*.] The aforementioned Greek word aggĕlŏs is the original word translated here as "angels."[23] The word "bosom" in "Abraham's Bosom," is the Greek word:

> "2859 kŏlpŏs; appar. a prim. word; the *bosom*; by anal. a *bay*: - bosom, creek."[24]

At this juncture the relationship between kŏlpŏs as a *bosom*, and/or a *bay* or *creek* is unclear.

Acts 27: 39 tells us:

> "And when it was day, they knew not the land:
> but they discovered a certain creek with a shore,
> into the which they were minded,
> if it were possible, to thrust in the ship."[25]

Here the original Greek word translated as *creek* is also kŏlpŏs.[26] The context here seems to be that kŏlpŏs is an area of *protection* for the "ship." This would seem to be consistent with the idea of the "bosom" of Abraham likewise offering *protection* for Lazarus. This sounds a bit like the previous "Limbus Patrum." The question here is protection specifically from what?

Meanwhile, RM: *"was buried; and in hell he lift up his eyes, being in torments, and seeth Abraham afar off, and Lazarus in his bosom."*

A cursory read of this, is that there is a clear distinction being made here that these two individuals are in separate areas, but separate areas of the same "location;" e.g.; both are in hell, but one is in the "air conditioned section," and protected by Abe. This was at a time when salvation via justification was not yet available.

[Given that a single Bible passage out of context is generally a pretext, nevertheless the following in Luke 13:28 is provided only as possible supportive evidence]:

> "There shall be weeping and gnashing of teeth,
> when ye shall see Abraham, and Isaac, and Jacob,
> and all the prophets, in the kingdom of God,
> and you yourselves thrust out."[27]

The actual Greek word translated as "hell" in this "Lazarus and the Rich Man" story in Luke 16:23 is:

"*86 hadēs*; from 1 (as a neg. particle) and *1492*; prop. *unseen*, i.e. "*Hades*" or the place (state) of departed souls: - grave, hell."[28] The "neg. particle" is "1 A a; of Heb. or.; The *first* letter of the alphabet; fig. only (from its use as a numeral) the first: - Alpha..."[29]

The root of *hadēs* that is negated is:

"*1492 ĕidō*; a prim verb; used only in certain past tenses, in the others being borrowed from the equiv. *3700* and *3708*; prop. to *see* (lit. or fig.); by impl. (in the perf. only) to *know*: - be aware, behold, x can (+ not tell), consider, (have) know (-ledge), look (on), perceive, see, be sure, tell, understand, wist, wot. Comp. 3700."[30]

So the literal definition of *hadēs* or Hades or hell in this translation is the *negation* of "to see;" or perhaps better stated as *not to see*, to *not see*. Thus the root of *hadēs* is actually a verb, and not a noun. Based upon this, the "unseen place" seems to be a reasonable definition.

But yet we are told that the very next thing RM did after being in this "unseen place," was *to see*: "*he lift up his eyes, being in torments, and seeth Abraham afar off, and Lazarus in his bosom.*"

Thus *intra-hadēs* seeing is possible. Ergo; it must be the *extra-hadēs* seeing of *hadēs* and that which is within it that is not possible—at least under "normal" circumstances. What or where is it from which *hadēs* is not able to be seen? The *material* and/or the *immaterial* realms seem to be the only possible answers.

The "torments" here in "being in torments" is:

"*931 basanŏs*; perh. remotely from the same as *939* (through the notion of *going* to the bottom); a *touchstone*, i.e. (by anal.) *torture*: - torment."[31]

"*939 basis*; from *baino* (to walk); a pace ("base"), i.e. (by impl.) the foot: - foot."[32]

It seems a bit odd to translate basanŏs as "torments." Rather, it seems to be concerned with going to the bottom, arguably via *walking* at some pace. Perhaps this is non-literal as in: "walk the walk," or "walking with God;" but here meaning *sinful* behavior. And perhaps this also means "cast into the earth," because of this sinful; i.e. *evil* behavior. And a "touchstone" is a stone used to test for precious metals.

We are told that Abraham and Lazarus were "afar off" from RM. The actual Greek word translated as "afar off" is:

"*3113* makrŏthĕn; adv. from *3117*; *from a distance* or *afar.*"[33]

This seems to establish that at least *at that time*, there was some type of "distance" in this neither or nether world. Whether this is literal distance, or some other type of separation is not stated here. This separation was to keep "afar" those who would not have even been there had salvation been available at that time—those such as Abraham; from those for whom this was irrelevant. But it must be remembered that Abraham is likely no longer present there today.

1 Peter 4:6 (KJV) tells us:

> *"For this cause was the gospel preached also to them that are dead, that they might be judged according to men in the flesh, but live according to God in the spirit."*[34]

This passage of course is arguable; but if "them that are dead" refers to spiritual death; i.e.; those who were physically dead, but in this "area;" then "live according to God in the spirit," can reasonably be interpreted as spiritually alive, or being re-connected with God. And it must be remembered that "gospel" means "good news."

It is not known whether this "area" continues to exist for those who were never given the opportunity to accept salvation.

In Verse 24 of the Lazarus and the Rich Man story we are told *"And he cried and said, Father Abraham, have mercy on me, and send Lazarus, that he may dip the tip of his finger in water, and cool my tongue; for I am tormented in this flame."*
The "flame" in "tormented in this flame" is:

> "5395 phlŏx; from a prim. phlĕgō (to *flash* or *"flame"*); a *blaze*: - flame (-ing)."[35]

Although we are told from where phlŏx is derived, but we are not told here what phlŏx actually means.
And the "tormented" here is:

> "3600 ŏdunaō; from 3601; to *grieve*: - sorrow, torment."[36]

In Verse 26 of the story we are told: *"And beside all this, between us and you there is a great gulf fixed: so that they which would pass from hence to you cannot; neither can they pass to us, that would come from thence."*
The actual Greek word translated as "gulf" is:

> "5490 chasma; from a form of an obsol. prim. chaō (to *"gape"* or *"yawn"*); a *"chasm"* or *vacancy* (impassable *interval*): - gulf."[37] According to Strong, this is the only time *chasma* appears in the entire New Testament.

There is some additional interesting information provided here in verse 26:
This *chasma* or "great gulf" seems to be confirmation of *kŏlpŏs* as a general area of *protection* for that which is within the "bosom" of Abraham, and here in the particular offering protection for Lazarus. And some additional information about one purpose of this *chasma* is provided; as we are told: *"so that they which would pass from hence to you cannot; neither can they pass to us, that would come from thence."*
But unlike "stumbling" upon the "creek" as *kŏlpŏs* in the previously referenced Acts 27: 39; (*"they discovered a certain creek*

with a shore, into the which they were minded, if it were possible, to thrust in the ship"); this "great gulf" was "fixed."

The Greek word translated as "fixed" is:

> "4741 stērizō; from a presumed der. of 2476 (like 4731); to *set fast*, i.e. (lit.) to *turn resolutely* in a certain direction, or (fig.) to *confirm*."[38]

When was this *chasma* "great gulf" stērizō or "fixed" or "set fast?" We are not told. But what we were previously told about in Revelation 12:9, was the establishment of an "area" when: "*the great dragon was cast out, that old serpent, called the Devil, and Satan, which deceiveth the whole world: he was cast out into the earth, and his angels were cast out with him.*"

It would be easy to assume that this event was the time when this *chasma* "great gulf" was *stērizō* or "fixed" or "set fast." But this particular event; (casting into the earth) was in fact the establishment of *hadēs* or Hades, or hell, or the "unseen place;" and *was not* the establishment of any *kŏlpŏs* as an area of *protection*, or the "bosom" of Abraham; by stērizō or "fixing" this *chasma* or "great gulf."

Cause generally precedes *effect*. [This is stated with the understanding that *effects* themselves, are generally causes of something else, or other *effect*(s).] But the *cause* for the *effect* of the very first sin by man; necessarily *preceded* this sin. It is not known what this very first sin was. What is reasonably known, is that this event occurred long before the formation of Adam.

Satan and his *aggĕlŏs* or *messengers* or "*tidings* bringers;" "deceiveth" or planaō; ("to (prop. *cause to*) *roam* (from safety, truth, or virtue) the whole world," *before* they were cast out; and arguably were cast out because of this. And as would later also be the case with Adam, this planaō provided the impetus for sin by man.

Thus the need for salvation occurred *after*; even if less than a nanosecond after; this very first planaō.

As it reasonably reads, the establishment of *hadēs* or Hades, or hell, or the "unseen place;" was because of what was done by the "old serpent, called the Devil, and Satan," and "*his angels* (who) *were cast out with him."* This was a "place" to send the *cause* for the later *effect* of man sinning.

But the provision of a means of man obtaining salvation was a long way off. Thus it seems an area that would protect those who would otherwise have been saved had salvation been available, was established. In order to provide this *kŏlpŏs* as an area of *protection*, or "bosom;" this *chasma* or "great gulf" was stērizō or "fixed" or "set fast?" And as we are told this *chasma* was *makrŏthĕn*, or was "from a distance or afar" from the rest of *hadēs* or Hades, or hell, or the "unseen place." And we are told that because of this makrŏthĕn: *"they which would pass from hence to you cannot; neither can they pass to us, that would come from thence."*

Thus in addition to the *"two* "edges" or "borders" providing "doors" to this (neither or nether world or hell) area, with one concealing this area (nether world or hell) from the *immaterial* realm and preventing entrance to the same; and with the other concealing this area from the *material* realm and preventing entrance into the same; there is also this internal *chasma* "great gulf" *within* this nether or neither world.

A recap of Luke 16:27-31:

> *"Then he said, I pray thee therefore, father,*
> *that thou wouldest send him to my father's house:*
> *For I have five brethren; that he may testify unto them,*
> *lest they also come into this place of torment.*
> *Abraham saith unto him, They have Moses*
> *and the prophets; let them hear them.*
> *And he said, Nay, father Abraham:*
> *but if one went unto them from the dead,*
> *they will repent. And he said unto him,*
> *If they hear not Moses and the prophets,*
> *neither will they be persuaded,*
> *though one rose from the dead."*

Abraham does not in any way state whether (this particular) Lazarus could or could not be resurrected and sent to RM's family.

Instead; what Abraham says, is that it would not do any good—implying that this is a *possible*, but a *useless* action.

It must be asked if this establishes confirmation of the existence of a means to leave this *kŏlpŏs* as an area of *protection*, or "bosom;" and go to the material world. Or alternatively; that no such means exists, but Abraham merely stated the most pertinent reason. The way it is written, it *seems* that this is possible, but it is not actually confirmed.

One cannot avoid the humor contained the last sentence. *"If they hear not Moses and the prophets, neither will they be persuaded, though one rose from the dead"*—this statement about Lazarus of course to later be equally applicable to Jesus.

Comunicare con Quelli nel Seno

[Communicating With Those in the Bosom]

In 1 Samuel 28:11-14 we are told:

> "Then said the woman, Whom shall I bring up unto thee? And he said, Bring me up Samuel.
>
> "And when the woman saw Samuel, she cried with a loud voice: and the woman spake to Saul, saying, Why hast thou deceived me? for thou art Saul.
>
> "And the king said unto her, Be not afraid: for what sawest thou? And the woman said unto Saul, I saw gods ascending out of the earth. And he said unto her, What form is he of? And she said, An old man cometh up;

and he is covered with a mantle.

*"And Saul perceived that it was Samuel, and he stooped with his face to the ground, and bowed himself."*³⁹

Here this Saul; (one who would never change his name to Paul); had murdered all of the "necromancers;" or those who could communicate with and obtain information from the physically deceased. But now he needed information, so he disguised himself and went out to find one.

Saul then tells this necromancer to "bring up" Samuel, who was deceased. Samuel clearly qualified as a "Patrum." He was the Samuel for whom this very book of the Bible was named; although it is unknown who actually wrote it.

It is interesting that this woman knew how to "bring up" Samuel, but it is not clear that she knew *who* it was (other than his name) that she "brought up." But once she "brought him up" she did know that the *disguised* man was Saul. Perhaps Samuel somehow had told her this, but this also is not clear.

The woman saw "gods ascending out of the earth." According to Strong, the original text was "see a god."⁴⁰

The Hebrew word translated here as "Gods" is:

> "430 'ĕlôhîym; plur. of 433: *gods* in the ordinary sense but spec. used (in the plur. thus, esp. with the art.) of the supreme *God*; occasionally applied by way of *deference* to *magistrates*; and sometimes as a superlative..."⁴¹

But it is unclear if this is the original word, or if it was also changed when the translation was changed.

It is also interesting that Saul asked her: "What form is he of?" The word "form" here is:

"8389 tô'ar; from 8388; *outline*, i.e. *figure* or *appearance*..."⁴²

Saul had murdered those with "familiar spirits," likely because he believed them to be not of God. So he likely was extremely skeptical regarding *who* or *what* it would be that this woman would "bring up;" quite likely expecting something demonic. It seems clear that although the woman actually *saw* some type of apparition of Samuel, Saul did not. But when Saul "perceived" that it was actually Samuel, he humbled himself.

The story again continues in 1 Samuel 28:15-16:

"And Samuel said to Saul,
Why hast thou disquieted me,
to bring me up?

"And Saul answered, I am sore distressed;
for the Philistines make war against me,
and God is departed from me,
and answereth me no more,
neither by prophets, nor by dreams:
therefore I have called thee,
that thou mayest make known unto me
what I shall do.

"Then said Samuel, Wherefore
then dost thou ask of me,
seeing the Lord is departed from thee,
and is become thine enemy?"⁴³

Here it seems Samuel is both inquiring and rebuking Saul. "Why are you bothering me?" would be a fair translation today. And Saul tells Samuel that this is because God doesn't answer him anymore. Saul mentions the prophets and the dreams, but not the Urim. Likely he does not want Samuel to know that even the High Priest cannot help him. Saul then tells Samuel that he needs "info" from him, so he knows *"what I shall do."* And Samuel then essentially asks Saul, "why ask me;" since the Lord departed from you and has become your enemy?

If it can be stipulated that Samuel was likely one who was in this "air conditioned" section of hell, or this nether or neither (unseen) world; within this *kŏlpŏs* as an area of *protection*, or "bosom;" then it is clear that Lazarus doing the same as Samuel, but at the behest of Abraham was possible.

The issue here is whether or not there is an opening from this *kŏlpŏs* as an area of *protection*, or "bosom;" to the material realm. The fact is that Samuel was *summoned* from this *kŏlpŏs* realm *to* the material realm; but RM wanted Lazarus *dispatched* from this *kŏlpŏs* realm *to* the material realm seems irrelevant with respect to the existence of the opening.

There seem to be a total of four openings from hell, this x-realm, or neither, or no realm:

The *first* is the aforementioned opening from the *immaterial* realm to this general "unchasmed" area (hell). This is the route by which Satan & Co. were sent there at the establishment of the same. This opening must continue to exist, or no one could else enter into "hell." The opening in this border or barrier is likely immaterial, and under God's control. It is unclear if this opening is, or ever was a "two-way" opening. This possibility will be addressed later.

The *second* is the previously addressed opening from this general area (hell), to the *material* realm. It is through this opening that that the enemy (as *nâchâsh* or hisser) managed to get to Adam & Co. in the *material gan* or guarded area, (often translated as garden) in Eden; to Jesus after His fasting; to Jesus in Gethsemane; as well as the enemy's other material "appearances."

And again it seems man has jurisdiction and control over this opening of this barrier *into the material world*, no matter what its composition—and irrespective of whether man is aware of this at any given time or not.

The *third* is the opening from this *kŏlpŏs* as an area of *protection*, or "bosom;" to the *immaterial* realm. This must necessarily be a "two-way" opening, as the very purpose of the establishment of this area, was to permit exit from this "subdivision of hell" and entry into the immaterial realm upon the availability of salvation via justification at a later time.

The *fourth* is the opening from this *kŏlpŏs* as an area of *protection*, or "bosom;" to the *material* realm. Saul and Samuel proved the existence of this opening into the material realm. This is likely a two-way opening, although we are not actually told what happened to Samuel after conversing with Saul.

It is difficult to understand these concepts of a "neither" realm; and the barriers or edges of this "area." It is even more difficult to understand the concept of openings in these barriers, from this "neither realm" to the two respective realms. Thus there is a constant attempt by man to "realize" this "area" as though it were a physical area—"into the physical earth" then meaning literally materially within the physical earth, along with whatever else is physically present.

But Revelation 20:14 tells us:

> "And death and hell were cast into the lake of fire. This is the second death."[44]

The original Greek word translated as "hell" in this passage is the aforementioned Hades.[45] Thus if "into the earth" meant *materially* or *physically* into the earth, then this same material part of earth would necessarily likewise have to be cast into this "lake of fire."

Luke 10:19 tells us:

> "Behold, I give unto you power to tread on serpents and scorpions, and over all the power of the enemy: and nothing shall by any means hurt you."[46]

The key phrase here is "over all the power of the enemy." This is one reason why the "Phantom Verse" Matthew 17:21, and its counterpart in Mark; were likely added by the enemy.

Clearly we are being told here in Luke that the enemy must obey the will of man. But this was stated by Jesus to those 70 "disciples" present; and it was *these* who here represented the "you." It remains unclear as to what other person or persons could be included in the group "you." The significance of this will be addressed in greater detail later.

But we are not told here that man has power over all the power of any *man* or *men*. Man is born with free will. So the truth, is that the most Abraham could have done was *asked* Lazarus to visit the RM's family.

La Fisica Dell'attività Demoniaca

[The Physics of Demonic Activity]

"In the physical science of electricity, one of the most fundamental laws is Ohm's Law; expressed as **E=IR**.

Here **E** is Electromotive force or voltage; **I** is the current, flow of electrons or Intensity; and **R** is the Resistance to that flow.

This law describes the relationship of the simple circuit. In order for current to flow, there must be: a current or movement of electrons; a force driving that current; and a load through which to drive it. As stated in this law: the larger the driving force (E), the greater the amount of electron flow through a given resistance or load (I); and the greater the resistance (R), the lesser amount of electron flow for a given force.

Ohm's law is a material law; and like all material laws, there is a corresponding law in the immaterial from which it came. One example of this law in the immaterial; relates to the intentions and actions of the enemy to supplant that which is in, or is of; the image and likeness of God; with that which is of him—that is; that which is not of God but is of the enemy.

That which is of him (the enemy) and not of Him, is analogous to the current. The enemy needs to get his current to flow into the hosts. As in an electrical circuit, once the current gets into the hosts; then changes begin.

The enemy does this in two very basic ways with respect to this **E=IR** law; both attempting to use forces, but with different tactical; (but the same strategic); intentions.

Firstly; he does this by the utilization of forces against the hosts that are analogous to voltage. He "cranks up" this voltage in order to get current to flow from him to the hosts. Much "actionable intelligence" can be gained by carefully observing the nature of these "voltage increases." This is because unlike voltage, there is a subjective component. What would be low voltage to one host, can be the same as high voltage to another; and vice versa. (This can often be the reason for what seems to be pettiness.) These forces are custom designed to produce the maximum voltage, (and ultimately maximum current flow); *for that particular host*; and thus there is much intelligence that can be obtained by the design and timing of the attack—but it also must be remembered that the enemy is not always correct.

However; just as in Ohm's law, in order for this to work, there must be the load, and that load of course is the host. But being made in the image and likeness of God; that load (host) is not a particularly good *conductor* for the enemy's "current." This necessarily means that the host *is* a particularly good *resistor*. In order to maximize the current flow for a given voltage; the enemy will also attempt to lower the host's resistance. Here also much "actionable intelligence" can be gained by carefully observing the nature of these attempts at lowering resistance; as the enemy will attack those areas he or it perceives as weak. But again, it must be remembered that the enemy is not always correct.

Job 1:10 tells us:

> *"Hast not thou made an hedge about him, and about his house, and about all that he hath on every side? thou hast blessed the work of his hands, and his substance is increased in the land."*[21]

Here Satan is complaining to God that He has "made an (sic.) hedge" around Job. This "hedge" results in increased resistance. And according to Ohm's law, increased resistance means less current flow, for a given voltage. Satan is essentially complaining here that the resistance is way too high, and he cannot get significant current to flow into Job. But he admits here that God is the one who "made" this hedge.

This "hedge" is actually:

> "7753 sûwk a prim. root; to *entwine*, i.e. *shut* in (for formation, protection or restraint):- fence, (make an) hedge (up)."[22]

This may seem unrelated at first, but is in fact quite relevant:

When God refers to "keeping" His commandments; most believe that "keep" or "keeping" means obey.

Here the actual Hebrew word is:

"shâmar; to hedge (about as with thorns), i.e. guard; ..."[23] [See MeekRaker Monograph #601 "Shâmar to Sharia"]

Here God is not talking about obedience; but *protecting* His commandments with a hedge. To the extent that this hedge is built; this also increases the host's resistance, also making the enemy's current flow to the host difficult. This is similar to the hedge around Job; but here this hedge or the act of *shâmar* must be *chosen* to be made by *man*.

A fair argument can be made that in a sense, this "God made" hedge or *sûwk* in the case of Job, is or was primarily for the material; and the "man made" hedge or *shâmar* is for the immaterial. It could further be argued that this "God made" hedge varied with action; and the "man made" hedge varies with thoughts.

As this "hedgeogenic" resistance increases; either less current will flow, or the enemy must somehow "crank up" the voltage. And there are limits; albeit sometimes changeable; to the "voltages" available to him.

What about the hosts not merely maximizing the resistance, but also affecting the voltage applied by the enemy? Paul told us how to do the former in Ephesians 6:10-17. However unbeknownst to many, he also told us how to do the latter; but since it is a short phrase which appears at the end of a lengthy passage concerning numerous defensive measures, it generally goes unnoticed. What is important is that when this offensive measure is utilized; and this *cannot* be overemphasized; *it should never be combined with anything that is of the enemy.*

Ephesians 6:17 tells us:

"And take the helmet of salvation,

and the sword of the Spirit, which is the word of God:"²⁴

Tucked in at the very end of the list of defensive (increasing resistance) measures in the preceding verses, and ending here in verse 17 after the last "and;" something rather interesting appears. In fact; therein lies a "bomb." And it is a rather interesting and quite powerful "bomb;"—the same representing the provision of a key instruction: *"(take) the sword of the Spirit, which is the word of God."*

This instruction is the only *offensive* (voltage lowering) instruction given in these verses.

What does "(take) the sword of the Spirit, which is the word of God" mean?

The actual Greek word translated as "sword" is:

> *"3162 machaira; prob. fem. of a presumed der. of 3163; a knife, i.e. dirk; fig. war, judicial punishment: - sword."*²⁵

As can be seen, the translation as "sword" is misleading. A dirk is not a sword. "Knife" or "Dagger" would be a better translation. These are designed for "up close and personal" combat. This is important because this (close up and tailor made), is precisely how the enemy attacks.

The figurative meaning should also be noted, that of "judicial punishment." There is an old saying: "Don't stick your head in the boxing ring if you don't want to get punched." It is the enemy who chooses to institute an attack. If the result is encountering a counterattack with a dirk, and he/it leaves a bit "bloodied," then he or it deserved it. But again, this should never be combined with anything that is of the enemy such as anger, hatred, etc. It is justice; ("judicial punishment"), and not vengeance that should be sought. If that which is of the enemy is at any time utilized, this can then easily be utilized by the enemy as a foothold.

The actual Greek word translated as "spirit" is:

> "*4151* pněuma; from *4154*; a *current* of air, i.e. *breath* (*blast*) or a *breeze*; by anal. or fig. a *spirit*, i.e. (human) the rational *soul*, (by impl.) *vital principle*, mental *disposition* etc..."[26]

Thus; "the knife of the soul" is a better translation. And precisely what is this "knife of the soul?"

It is the "word of God." What is this word? The actual Greek "word" translated here as "word" is:

> "*4487* rhēma; from *4483*; an *utterance* (individ., collect. or spec.); by impl. a *matter* or *topic* (espec. of narration, command or dispute); with a neg. *naught* whatever..."[27]

John 1:1 tells us:

> *"In the beginning was the Word, and the Word was with God, and the Word was God."*[28]

However the actual word translated here three times as "word" is not rhēma, but rather:

> "*3056* lŏgŏs; from *3004*; something *said* (including the *thought*); by impl. a *topic* (subject of discourse), also *reasoning* (the mental faculty) or *motive*; by extens. a

> *computation*; spec. (with the art. In John) the Divine *Expression* (i.e. *Christ*)..."[29]

So it must be asked what is the difference between rhēma and lŏgŏs; and why was rhēma used by Paul, and lŏgŏs used in John?

Paul was giving instructions for *future* behavior, and John was recollecting *past* events. Thus rhēma; meaning an *utterance*; refers to what God *is* or *will be* saying "real time." Lŏgŏs refers to what God has or had already said.[47] [Excerpt from *"Its Not Just A Theory,"* also included in the pentalogy: *"Wisdom Essentials."* Copyright © 2017 Quadrakoff Publications Group, LLC All rights reserved.]

Thus we have both defensive and offensive measures against the enemy. Here "the enemy" refers to Satan himself, as well as any "angels" or aggĕlŏs, seeking "planaō; or again: "to (prop. *cause to*) *roam* (from safety, truth, or virtue): - go astray, deceive, err, seduce, wander, be out of the way."

It matters little what the immaterial *structure* any particular aggĕlŏs may have. It is their *function* as immaterial messengers, or bringing tidings deliberately in order to obtain planaō, that puts all of these under man's control. Many of these may not in any way resemble the immaterial structure; whatever that actually means; of Gabe or Mike; but if they are aggĕlŏs as defined; *and* they are seeking planaō, this alone is sufficient.

True aggĕlŏs, or those aggĕlŏs who obey the will of God; i.e.; those not seeking planaō; must likewise obey the will of man, as long as man's will does not conflict with the will of God.

However, when man's will conflicts with the will of God, true aggĕlŏs must defer to the will of God even though this may conflict with man's will. To do otherwise would constitute actions or inactions in furtherance of planaō. And we are told what happens when aggĕlŏs engage in planaō.

Danté Camminatore

L'enigma

[The Conundrum]

By definition, the *material* realm has time, space and matter. Depending upon their "persuasion;" most describe the "Big Bang," or Genesis 1:1, or both; as the very *creation* via bârâ', or utilizing "no-thing;" of time, space, and matter.

Ergo; as previously stated, the *immaterial* realm has no time, no space, and no matter. Although invisible, "material" radio waves obey the "inverse square law" with regard to wave intensity. Radio is considered as an electromagnetic phenomenon, and electrons do in fact have mass; albeit a rather small amount of mass—believed to be a mere 9.109×10^{-31} kg. Radio "waves" travel at roughly the speed of light—most assuredly way too slow for any future intergalactic communications from many other 'erets or "firm" places.

But purely *immaterial* phenomena such as *telepathy* do not obey these material rules. And whether it is "a psychic," (information about the past or future); or "a clairvoyant" ("real time" information); neither function is subject to this inverse square law, nor any speed of light limitations. This is why science fiction writers often write about utilizing telepaths for travel light years from earth, as material phenomena such as radio would simply take too long. By definition a radio signal transmitted from a celestial body one hundred light years away, would likewise require one hundred years to reach the earth; and another 100 years for any response to be received.

Thus it would seem that there is no possible duration or sequencing of events from the *immaterial* perspective. Yet we know this is not so from the *material* perspective. What God did in terms of redemptive acts for the earth, after the condition of the earth described as per Genesis 1:2; (after the "without form and void"); was *sequential* from the material perspective—whether *yom* is translated as *chiros* (period of activity); or *kronos* (the "literal day" translation).

When Gabriel visited Mary there was *material* duration before he visited Joseph, to let Joseph know Mary had not "cheated on him." But one must ask what this "duration" between these two events from the immaterial realm was; given that time does not exist in that realm? The same could be asked with regard to distance.

Reconciling these time and distance "paradoxes" between the two realms with respect to events; is extremely difficult, if not impossible. From the *immaterial* perspective it seems that everything must happen simultaneously and in the same place. But clearly this is not so from the *material* perspective.

We are left with only three possible "places" for "a thing" to be:

Any *material* or "firm" "thing;" including the material part of a "living or dual being such as man (body or *soma*), exists on the material realm and is subject to material or "natural" law. When any material "thing" disobeys natural law, this is referred to as a *miracle*.

The material part of that which is called physical "life," in essence represents an ongoing defying of natural law or a miracle—irrespective of the fact that it is seldom considered as such. When physical "life" ends with the last breath; and the immaterial part "leaves" the body; natural law takes over with that which "remains;" just as is normally the case with those material "things" that never "lived." A "living" thing consistently violates natural law when "alive" within certain limitations. And when disconnected from this immaterial part, natural law then prevails over that which is material.

If it is a "legitimate" *immaterial* "thing," it exists primarily on the immaterial realm—*legitimate* here meaning neither previously being "thrown out;" nor refused re-admittance because of contamination. [It is not clear whether any of these individual immaterial "thrown out" entities can obtain re-admittance via salvation. It is quite possible that this was the reason behind the Biblical inclusion of the story of "Legion"—more about this later.]

Existing on the immaterial realm does not preclude activities that cause changes on the material realm from that (the immaterial) realm. This is precisely what God did in early Genesis after the creation of the realm as described in Genesis 1:1. Genesis 1:1 does not count, as this was the *establishment* of the material realm.

And since; at least according to God in Genesis 2:7; man has an *immaterial* component, he is capable of causing change in the *immaterial* realm; as well as "indirectly" causing changes to the *material* realm, via the immaterial realm. This is one purpose for prayer. This is to be distinguished from making *direct* material changes to that which is in the material realm. The immaterial portion of man via *will* is also the major contributor to equal and opposite reactions, or that which is often considered as *karma*. (See the Monograph *"Inevitable Balance"*)

But again there is also that X area, that area which is immaterial in nature, but not a part of the immaterial realm—that *neither* or *nether* world; AKA: *hell*.

How did this happen? There are things that are known, and things that are unknown. Clearly when the previously cited passage Revelation 12:7-9 (KJV) tells us: *"And there was war in heaven: Michael and his angels fought against the dragon; and the dragon fought and his angels, And prevailed not; neither was their place found any more in heaven. And the great dragon was cast out, that old serpent, called the Devil, and Satan, which deceiveth the whole world: he was cast out into the earth, and his angels were cast out with him;"*—this represents or represented a change, or changes.

In scientific notation, change is represented by the Greek letter delta or Δ. Here we are told of a Δ in that which was *contained* in the immaterial realm. Likewise there must also have been some corresponding Δ in wherever it was that the enemy and his "angels" were "cast out into."

As previously addressed, this *"cast out into the earth, and his angels were cast out with him;"* likely represents the actual establishment of this quarantined area or *neither* world, *nether* world, or *hell*.

But what was the reason for, or *cause* of this Δ? In inquiring as to what was the cause for this Δ, *distinctions* must be made. The enemy and his "angels" being "cast out" for what they did or did not do; is entirely different than *why* or *how* it is that they did or did not do the same. The specifics (their actions or inactions); or the reason(s), or why they were *cast out*, thus being different than why there was a *war*.

So there are actually three concerns. Firstly is the introduction of "evil;" or that being what is against God's will into the immaterial realm. Second would be the result, or that which was facilitated by this introduction of evil, or the *cause* of or for the war. And third is the war itself, and the results of the same.

#1 Evil Introduced → #2 Evil Actions → #3 War and Expulsion

or

Δ Immaterial Contents → Δ Behavior → Δ Location

The #1 or the introduction of the evil to the immaterial realm, is perhaps the greatest secret "unknown to man." But these passages in Revelation do in fact provide a reasonable answer for #2 and #3.

The *"which deceiveth the whole world"* represents an evil action that may have necessitated or caused the war. Much like being contaminated by sin, the magnitude of the contamination is largely irrelevant, as *no* amount of evil can be permitted to exist on the immaterial realm. And all along man thought it was he, and not He, who had invented "zero tolerance" policies.

From the *material* standpoint, this is somewhat analogous to Adam's time in the *gan*, or protected area, usually translated as garden. Once the enemy showed up (H. nâchâsh or hisser), sinful behavior began, and expulsion was necessary.

If this "deceiveth" was in any way the reason or even part of the reason for this war and expulsion, it logically follows that the enemy necessarily must have engaged in this while still in the immaterial realm.

And not only was the enemy banished from the immaterial realm, but also were "his angels." What were his "angels" doing prior to the war and expulsion? "Well you know angels can do lots of things."

But as previously noted, word translated as "angels" in this passage is: "32 aggĕlŏs; from aggĕllō;... (to *bring tidings*); a *messenger*; esp. an "*angel*"; by impl. a *pastor*:- angel, messenger."

And again these particular aggĕlŏs sought and seek "4105 planaō;... to (prop. *cause to*) *roam* (from safety, truth, or virtue): - go astray, deceive, err, seduce, wander, be out of the way."

The *means*, is or are, aggĕlŏs, via *messages* or *tidings*; and the *ends*, is or are planaō, or "*cause to roam* (from safety, truth, or virtue).

And as also previously addressed, the definition of the aggĕlŏs, or to be a tidings bringer or messenger, requires three things:

- One who sent a message or tidings;
- the message or tidings, itself or themselves;
- a recipient for the message or tidings.

It seems reasonable to conclude that it was the enemy; "*called the Devil, and Satan*;" and his minions who were the sources of the messages, and/or those who sent the messages or tidings.

There is no information presented in these passages regarding what information or disinformation these messages actually contained. What we are told however, is that whatever they were, they were in furtherance of an act or acts of *deception or planaō*.

We are not told that the enemy *attempted* to deceive, but rather that he "deceiveth," or in fact was or were successful at some level of deception or *planaō*.

It must be remembered here that there are three ways of lying. The *first* way is the outright lie. The *second* is to tell the truth, but only part of it: ["Four men broke into a home and abducted a child who later died. What do you think should happen to them? Oh, I forgot to tell you that they were firemen, the house was on fire; and the child later died from previous smoke inhalation."] And the *third* is to tell the complete truth, but in such a manner that the recipient is certain it is a lie, and believes the opposite: "Yeah right, I did it."

It must be noted that with regard to these particular machinations of the enemy, nothing has changed to this very day; except perhaps his location, and level of power.

But of course it must be determined who the intended *recipients* of these messages in fact were, as the "whole world" represents a rather large number of possibilities.

In diagnosing a cardiac murmur or an "abnormal heart sound;" the first thing generally done is to determine *where* in the cardiac cycle this murmur presents itself. Likewise in determining precisely *who* it was that was being deceived, and also *when* it was that this deception was occurring with regard to these passages; the timing of these events described in Revelation 12:7-9 should be "synched" with what if anything it was that was happening (concurrently) on the material realm. And of course although a lot of "funky" things may also have been happening on Pluto and the Moon at the same time; it seems that it is the "whole world;" i.e.; the earth; both at this time and before the expulsion, that should be the primary concern.

Why is this important? Because it is important to understand what happened in the past, in order to not make the same mistakes in the future. The enemy continues to "deceiveth," irrespective of his "location."

Most consider Genesis 1:2 to be a continuation of Genesis 1:1. Specifically that these passages represent a description of a multi-part process. Specifically; that first God created the earth, as stated in Genesis 1:1; and *then* He continued the process of creating the earth, in order to create the earth already described as completed at the end of Genesis 1:1. This "view" requires many things: including that the "earth" we are told was created at the end of Genesis 1:1 was not in fact the earth, but rather some *"pre-earth* mass."

Following is Genesis 1:1-2 (KJV):

> *"In the beginning God created the heaven
> and the earth.
> And the earth was without form, and void;
> and darkness was upon the face of the deep.
> And the Spirit of God moved upon the face of the waters."*[48]

"MeekRaker Beginnings..." devotes the first four chapters to this and other related matters. Following is a short excerpt:

> "It seems reasonable; that in the beginning, God created the heavens and the earth just as the book states, and not chaos or a deep or a pre-earth mass. Then something happened which made the earth without form (or formless) and void; that after all being the way it reads. Most translations and versions do not actually state *"and then,"* but that is the only explanation that seems to make any degree of sense. Although it must be stated, that the *Interlinear* version on *Scripture4all.org* does include in their translation: "she (the earth) became.""[1.5][49]

So first, decisions must be made as to precisely what was going on in Genesis 1:2:

Is Genesis 1:1 *incorrect* by concluding that the earth was created? If this is so, and that it was actually some pre-earth mass that was in fact *created*, then this presents many substantial problems.

One such problem; is that the word "creation" is actually the Hebrew *bârâ'*, which requires that *nothing material* be utilized in the bringing of a material "thing" into existence.

If this position is taken; specifically that "In the Beginning" God did not actually create or bârâ' the *earth* as we are told He did; but instead He created or *bârâ'* some "pre-earth mass," which would only later then *become* the earth; then some process other than the use of creation or *bârâ'*; is required—perhaps *yâtsar* as in the *formation* of Adam; or *bânâh* as in the *fashioning* of Eve. "

And with this position, "*And the Spirit of God moved upon the face of the waters*," would then mean that this "movement" was a necessary part of this *creation* process. And thus whatever represents these "waters," had to materially exist as this "pre-earth mass" *prior* to the end of the "creation" process, in order for anything to "move upon." But again this would not be *creation* or *bârâ'* as we are clearly told the process was in Genesis 1:1.

Or; is Genesis 1:1 *correct* as written by concluding that it was the earth that was bârâ' or created? If this is so, and that it was not actually some pre-earth mass that was created, but rather the earth as stated; then this means that the completed earth somehow "became" in the condition that it was as described in Genesis 1:2.

If Genesis 1:1 is *correct* as written, and the earth then "became" without form and void; could it be that perhaps God simply changed His mind? Thus here it would have been *God* Himself who then was the *cause* for this *effect* or change in the earth *from* that which was described at the conclusion of Genesis 1:1, *to* that which is described in Genesis 1:2.

This makes little sense; not only because many believe that God does not (or cannot) actually change His mind; but also because in addition; *if* it was God who made these changes, it must be asked not only *why* he changed His mind; but also why He then expended so much effort to restore the earth back to what it was at the end of Genesis 1:1—including later creating man as tsâbâ or hosts in order to "put the kibosh on (H. tsâbâ and kâbash are God's own words via Moses)" the earth? This would also then necessarily mean that God changed His mind yet once again.

Most Bible "experts" agree that the Bible is not a history book, but rather a book about *redemption*. The problem is that they generally do not realize the magnitude of what these words actually mean. From man's self-centered viewpoint, this "redemption" is usually considered to refer strictly to the redemption of man. "The first adam," (Adam); provided the bloodline for "the last adam," (Jesus). "And so accept the salvation and 'you're done.'" Of course the redemption of man is important, and that is beyond question. But it seems there is much more going on here.

What is *reasonably* known; is that the condition of the earth changed dramatically *from* what it was at the end of Genesis 1:1; *to* what it had become at the beginning of Genesis 1:2. We also know that at some point the enemy and his *aggĕlŏs*, or messengers or "tidings bringers" were cast out of the immaterial realm because they "*deceiveth the whole world*"—necessarily while they were still in that immaterial realm.

We also know that God began the redemptive process, but then created man as tsâbâ, usually translated as "hosts," in order to kâbash (Hebrew), or "put the kibosh" (English) on the earth, in order to continue the redemptive process. If it is stipulated that this is so; it must be asked why God didn't finish the job himself; but instead creating tsâbâ, and over time providing a book about "redemption?"

> "Although this is also beyond the scope of this work, the latter (absolute sense), strongly suggests some type of "life form(s)" be present on the earth between Genesis 1:1 and Genesis 1:2—else what was the target of the deception? What God actually and literally did during that which is known as the "creation," (as opposed to and after conclusion of the "beginning") is consistent with this possibility. Most believe that early Genesis is fraught with "creating." However an unbiased analysis of the actual events based upon actual terminology, strongly suggests otherwise.

"Words mean things, and perfect synonyms are difficult, especially in translations. Actually, it is not certain that there are any perfect synonyms within the same language. In the beginning, it was the heavens and the earth that was created. In fact, the terms "created" or "creature," do not appear again in Genesis until verses 21 and 20 respectively."[5.5]

"This would also be consistent with the concept of beliefs regarding an Atlantis or Lemuria—at least in terms of *some* life forms being present at that time (between Genesis 1:1 and 1:2; or between the words "earth" and "without form and void"). Those who scoff at this idea, generally claim ignorance of plate tectonics on the part of the proponents, as the reason for this belief. However; although "evidence" regarding the timeframe is sketchy at best; *if* some type of continent such as Atlantis existed, it existed at a time between one million and one hundred million years ago—chronologically long before the *created* hosts and the kibosh directive, and even longer before the *formation* of A & E. The "plates" can move substantially in one hundred million years. If something similar to Atlantis existed, it is generally believed to ultimately have become covered in water. If this sounds familiar to those who understand early Genesis, there are very good reasons for this familiarity."[50]

Just prior to the above, it was asked: "Why God didn't finish the job himself; but instead created tsâbâ, and then over time providing a book about redemption?" The answer is that He could not.

"But God can do anything." The truth is that God can do anything that can be done, no matter how difficult or impossible it may seem. But God cannot do that which cannot be done. God cannot set up a system where two means two when one is writing a check, but two means fifty million when depositing this same check written in the same amount. The quantity two must remain two—

no matter how much God or anyone else would like it to be different in some particular circumstances. If He did not maintain this, it is likely that the entire universe would either explode or collapse. This is not to say that the same result cannot be achieved; but merely that it would have to in some way be balanced, or "paid for."

If there were beings on the earth between Genesis 1:1 and Genesis 1:2, these could have provided the *targets* for the deceptions by the *aggĕlŏs*, or messengers, or "tidings bringers; seeking planaō; from 4106; to (prop. *cause to*) *roam* (from safety, truth, or virtue): - go astray, deceive, err, seduce, wander, be out of the way."

And the ultimate result was the condition of the earth as described in the beginning of Genesis 1:2: "without form and void."

What is it that is known that cannot *reasonably* be controverted?

- The enemy and his *aggĕlŏs* were originally in the immaterial realm.
- The enemy and his *aggĕlŏs* engaged in *planaō* while in the immaterial realm.
- For some reason, likely because of this *planaō*, there was a war in the immaterial realm between Michael, and the enemy and these *planaō* seeking *aggĕlŏs*; and the enemy and his *aggĕlŏs* lost.
- Because they lost, the enemy and his *aggĕlŏs*, were cast out of the immaterial realm, and "into the earth."
- The targets of the *planaō* was the earth (whole world), and thus any living beings upon the earth at that time.
- The earth must have already been created at this time, else what would there have been to *planaō* or deceiveth; and furthermore how could one be cast into something that did not yet exist?
- Thus this casting out had to occur after Genesis 1:1.
- The enemy was clearly on the earth by Genesis 3:1, as he appears in Genesis 3:1-5 (KJV): "*Now the serpent was more subtil than any beast of the field which the LORD God had made. And he said unto the woman, Yea, hath God said, Ye*

shall not eat of every tree of the garden? And the woman said unto the serpent, We may eat of the fruit of the trees of the garden: But of the fruit of the tree which is in the midst of the garden, God hath said, Ye shall not eat of it, neither shall ye touch it, lest ye die. And the serpent said unto the woman, Ye shall not surely die: For God doth know that in the day ye eat thereof, then your eyes shall be opened, and ye shall be as gods, knowing good and evil."[51]

- But if the enemy had previously been cast *into the earth*, how was it that he was then capable of being *on the earth* while he was in the *gan* or garden? The answer is the aforementioned "door" from that no-realm, into the material realm.
- God was not content with the condition of the world in Genesis 1:2, as he began making substantial changes to it.
- God then *created* man in Genesis 1:26-28, as previously referenced; giving man the assignment and authority to "put the kibosh" on the earth—translated in the KJV as "subdue it, (the earth)."
- Since God is omnipotent, it cannot be the case that He was *unable* to finish the "kiboshing" Himself, as a matter of *power* or *capability*. This leaves simply lack of *authority* as the only possible reason God needed recourse via the created tsâbâ or hosts. It seems likely that God did not have this authority at the time, as He had already delegated the same to those in whom it was that were deceiveth prior to the creation of man, but then no longer existed on the earth. Thus the authority in Genesis 1:26-28 represents a *transfer* of this authority over the earth to the *created* hosts, rather than any initial *granting*.

In order to be precise, we reasonably know that the enemy's destination was "into the earth." Likely this was also the destination of his *aggĕlŏs*, or messengers, or "tidings bringers;" although we are not actually told this in—"*cast out into the earth, and his angels were cast out with him."* It is not actually stated here that the *aggĕlŏs* were also "cast *into the earth,"* but this seems likely.

In further support of this "into the earth" translation, examining what God told us as part of the "Commandments is illuminating."

"Exodus 20:4 (NAS) tells us:

> "You shall not make for yourself
> an idol, or any likeness
> of what is in heaven above
> or on the earth beneath or
> in the water under the earth."[10.17]

"The actual word for "under" is "8478 tachath, from the same as 8430; the *bottom* (as *depressed*); only adv. *below* (often with prep. pref. *underneath*), in *lieu of,* etc.: - as, beneath..."[10.18] So it is certain that "under" (or bottom or below) is a fair translation; and this time water means water, or at least a liquid.

"One might reasonably ask: "Precisely what is it that is or was in the water or liquid under the earth that one is not permitted to make a likeness of?" The answer of course presupposes that one knows what the water or liquid under the earth referred to actually is, or was, to begin with. This clearly does not refer to seas, lakes or other bodies of water that are on the surface of the earth, as they have earth beneath them and not above them. Thus these bodies of water or liquid are actually above the "earth," and not beneath.

"There do exist, of course, bodies of water beneath the earth. However, it can also be stated that far under solid ground, other types of liquids exist; and exist in much greater quantity. Actually, these liquids are such that they have a freezing point above the surface temperature of the earth. So, depending on ones perspective, it could be said that the earth is actually really a liquid, with a thick frozen crust "floating" on this liquid; with this crust or land being the surface upon which we live. The nature and temperature of these liquids can be seen with a volcanic eruption. The science of plate tectonics is based upon this.

"If God was referring to this liquid in Exodus 20:4, it clearly bears close resemblance to the common perception of hell."[52]

Most would believe that in the general sense, angels or aggĕlŏs are capable of much more that merely carrying messages or tidings. What must be remembered is the hierarchy: God, then man, then angels. As previously stated, angels are supposed to obey both man and God; with the understanding that when the will of man and the will of God conflict, it is God's will that prevails.

Are angels in the image and likeness of God? How could they not be, in that the creation must necessarily be a subset of that which is contained in its creator? This is why the origin of evil is not only so difficult to comprehend, but it is difficult to construct a working thesis as to the mechanism, without contradicting that which is known to be true. It is one thing to describe what happened when evil attempted to enter the immaterial realm or "heaven." It is another thing entirely to understand what happened prior to this event, and whence it came.

And as was the case with Adam, man being in the image and likeness of God in this original state; lacks even the *knowledge* of evil. And as was also the case with Adam, the knowledge of evil must be *brought* to man by the enemy. It is these messages or tidings seeking "planaō; from *4106*; to (prop. *cause to*) *roam* (from safety, truth, or virtue): - go astray, deceive, err, seduce, wander, be out of the way;" that are utilized in order to facilitate the *knowledge* of, and man's subsequent *choosing* of evil. This is the main method today by which the enemy manipulates man into making choices to the enemy's liking. Since as stated, man has the authority over all angels to the extent that man's will does not conflict with God's will; even aggĕlŏs seeking planaō cannot force man to do anything. Thus they are forced to lie.

But what other capabilities did or do these "banished" aggĕlŏs seeking planaō have other than "malignant jawboning?"

Danté Camminatore

Le Cose Erano Diverso Modo Indietro Allora

[Things Were Different Way Back Then]

In Exodus 7, God tells Moses to go with Aaron to tell Pharaoh to let the Israelites leave. God also states that Pharaoh will refuse, and Pharaoh will request that a miracle be performed. God then tells Moses to tell Aaron to cast his rod before Pharaoh, and it will become a serpent. This is all performed successfully.

Pharaoh, not to be outdone, "*called the wise men and the sorcerers: now the Magicians of Egypt,*"[53] who then perform essentially the very same "miracle."

At first blush it appears that there are two groups of individuals called in by Pharaoh. The first group is the *wise men*; and the second group is the *sorcerers*, which seems reasonable enough.

These "*wise men and the sorcerers: now the Magicians of Egypt,*" in the original Hebrew are:

"Wise men:" "2450 châkâm; from 2449; *wise*, (i.e. intelligent skilful (sic.) artful): - cunning (man), subtil ([un-]), wise ([hearted], man)."[54]

"The sorcerers:" "3784 kâshaph; a prim. root; prop. to *whisper* a spell, i.e. to *inchant* or practise (sic.) magic: - sorcerer, (use) witch (-craft).en."[55]

"Magicians:" "2748 charṭôm: from the same as 2747; a *horoscopist* (as *drawing* magical lines or circles): - magician."[56]

There is an obvious "disconnect" here with "wise men and the sorcerers: now the Magicians of Egypt;" as *châkâm* means *wise*, not "wise men;" and thus is an adjective. And *kâshaph* means "*to whisper* a spell;" and thus seems best characterized as a verb.

Thus literally pharaoh "called the wise and to whisper a spell: now the Magicians of Egypt," We don't reasonably get to a noun until *charṭôm*, and although it is translated as *magician*, it literally means *horoscopist*.

Although *horoscope* is generally associated with astrology, it actually literally refers to *looking* at, *seeing* or *watching* the *hour*; or some other period of time. Likewise since astrologers draw lines and circles on paper; there is a temptation to assume that this "horoscopic drawing" is limited to the astrological chart; and not the drawing of lines or circles elsewhere. But here the definition refers only to "*drawing* magical lines or circles," and does not specify where. A pentagram drawn on the ground is also comprised of lines; and a circle drawn on the ground likewise fits this definition.

So rather than two groups of individuals, literally there is but one; these *charṭôm* who are being characterized as wise or *châkâm*; who are capable of *kâshaph* or whispering spells.

It seems there soon will be a bit of a problem developing here, and not just because "*Aaron's rod swallowed up their rods.*"[57] The very same "duplication" then happens when God tells Moses to tell Aaron to turn all the water into blood, and Aaron does;

except since these *charṭôm* are now "rod-less," they now use "enchantments" only.⁵⁸

"Enchantments" here is:

> "3909 lâṭ; a form of 3814 or else part. from 3874: prop. *covered*, i.e. *secret*; by impl. *incantation*; also *secrecy* or (adv.) *covertly*: - enchantment, privily, secretly, softly."⁵⁹

And the same thing happens again with the frogs.

But when God commanded Moses to tell Aaron to bring forth lice with his rod, there is a different result:

Exodus 8:18-19 (KJV) tells us:

> *"And the magicians did so with their enchantments to bring forth lice, but they could not: so there were lice upon man, and upon beast. Then the magicians said unto Pharaoh, This is the finger of God: and Pharaoh's heart was hardened, and he hearkened not unto them; as the Lord had said."*⁶⁰

The Hebrew word translated as "finger of" is:

> "676 'etsba'; from the same as 6648 (in the sense of *grasping*); some thing to *seize* with, i.e. a *finger*; by anal. a *toe*: - finger, toe"⁶¹

The Hebrew word translated as "God" is:

> "430 'ĕlóhîym; plur. of 433; *gods* in the ordinary sense; but spec. used (in the plur. thus, esp. with the art.) of the supreme *God*; occasionally applied by way of deference to *magistrates*; and sometimes as a

superlative: - angels, x exceeding, God (gods) (-dess –ly), x (very) great, judges, x mighty."[62]

It is not only that these magicians or *charṭôm* failed in their attempts to "bring forth lice," but what is more important is *why* they failed. These *charṭôm* had "miraculous" capabilities, but only to a certain point. Clearly it was God who provided the power for Aaron to bring forth the lice, but when the *charṭôm* attempted this, they could not. And the reason they could not; at least according to these very same *charṭôm*; was because what Aaron had was the "finger" or the power of God. Ergo; these *charṭôm* had power; but their power was not of God.

If these *charṭôm* had such powers, albeit not unlimited and we are told they did; it must be asked what was the source of their (the *charṭôm)* power. Since by their own admission it was not of God; Hobson's choice tells us that it was: *"that old serpent, called the Devil, and Satan, which deceiveth the whole world: he was cast out into the earth, and his angels were cast out with him."* Unless of course there was somehow a third source—a proffering for which no evidence whatsoever exists.

It must be noted that it is unclear what type of power was utilized here. The way the passages read, it appears to be *bârâ'*; or again the bringing forth of a material thing utilizing nothing material. But given some of the original verbiage; it is not clear that it was in fact *bârâ'*, but perhaps *yâtsar* or *formation* as in the case of Adam; or *bânâh* or *fashioning* as in the case of Eve. This is supported by that fact that if early Genesis is correctly read, it seems that God only uses *bârâ'* one time when bringing a thing into existence—true creating. As though once a thing conceived in the immaterial and is brought into material existence, this *potential* is removed from the immaterial. Although this is clearly arguable, the preponderance of evidence supports this.

But what we do know, is that the *charṭôm* utilizing the powers of those entities who had been "cast out," did not have the power capabilities of Aaron. They admitted this, and stated why this was so. And many years later a serious problem for the power of *"that old serpent, called the Devil, and Satan, which deceiveth the whole world: he was cast out into the earth, and his angels were cast out with him"* would manifest. This of course being when Jesus "descended."

The fair conclusion is that prior to the "casting out," these entities likely had power equal to other angels. Then it seems their power was diminished at the time of, or at some time after their expulsion. And there was then a further diminution at Calvary. But of course *diminution* is not synonymous with removal.

Danté Camminatore

Angeli per Struttura

[Angels by Structure]

That which is immaterial and contains only that which is of God, resides in the immaterial; as opposed to residing in an "immaterial*oid*" *neither* realm or *nether* world. Angels or aggĕlŏs; [the non- *planaō* seeking, as the *planaō* seekers don't seem to "stick around" long]; are named such in the New Testament. They are named for *function* (messages and tidings), and not as a result of their *structure*. Thus any immaterial entity in the immaterial realm that is functioning in this manner could be considered angels or aggĕlŏs by this very definition. Even the Holy Ghost providing rhēma could be included in this strictly *functional* definition.

But what were angels called in the Old Testament?

"Angel" (singular) in the *Old Testament* is a translation of two similar Hebrew words. The most common is:

> "4397 mal'âk; from an unused root mean. to *dispatch* as deputy; a *messenger*; spec. of God, i.e. an *angel* (also a prophet, priest or teacher): - ambassador, angel, king, messenger."[63]

The other is a similar Hebrew word and appears only *twice* in the Old Testament, and *only* in Daniel. And it is the only Hebrew word in Daniel translated as "angel:"

> "4398 mal'ak (Chald.); corresp. to 4397; an *angel*: - angel."[64]

The most common word translated as "angels" (plural) in the Old Testament is also 4397.[65]

In Psalms there are two different Hebrew words translated as *angels* (plural); and one Hebrew word translated as *angels'* (plural possessive).

The first of the two Hebrew words in Psalms translated as "angels" is the same word used by the *charṭôm* when explaining their failure (as owner of the finger):

> "430 'ĕlôhîym; plur. of 433; *gods* in the ordinary sense; but spec. used (in the plur. thus, esp. with the art.) of the supreme *God*; occasionally applied by way of deference to *magistrates*; and sometimes as a superlative: - angels, x exceeding, God (gods) (-dess –ly), x (very) great, judges, x mighty."[66]

The second of the two Hebrew words in Psalms translated as "angels" is:

> "8136 shin'ân; from 8132; *change*, i.e. *repetition*: - x angels."[67]

The Hebrew plural possessive "angels'" is:

> "47 'abbîyr; for 46: - angel, bull, chiefest, mighty (one), stout [-hearted], strong (one), valiant."[68]

> "46 'âbîyr; from 82; *mighty* (spoken of God): - mighty (one)."[69]

"82 'âbar; a prim. root; to *soar*: - fly."⁷⁰

Surprisingly; according to Strong, the word "archangel" only appears twice in the entire Bible:
"Archangel" appears in 1 Thessolonians 4:16 (KJV):

> *"For the Lord himself shall descend from heaven with a shout, with the voice of the archangel, and with the trump of God: and the dead in Christ shall rise first;"*⁷¹

And "archangel" also appears in Jude 1:9:

> *"Yet Michael the archangel, when contending with the devil he disputed about the body of Moses, durst not bring against him a railing accusation, but said, The Lord rebuke thee."*⁷²

The original Greek word translated as "archangel" in both 1 Thessolonians 4:16 and in Jude 1:9 is:

"743 archaggĕlŏs; from 757 and 32; a *chief angel*: - archangel."⁷³

"757 is: "archō; a prim. verb; to be *first* (in political rank or power): - reign (rule) over."⁷⁴ applied to the previous aggĕlŏs.

What is interesting here is the inclusion of the *definite* article "the" in the translations of both of these passages: "the voice of *the* archangel" and "Michael *the* archangel (italics supplied)." This is to be distinguished from an indefinite article such as "an;" e.g.; the voice of *an* archangel, or Michael *an* archangel. This would lead one to believe that there exists only *one* archangel. And it must be asked precisely how many angels could be considered "to be first," as the definition of archō requires?

It was Michael who fought Satan: *"And there was war in heaven: Michael and his angels fought against the dragon."* It was Michael and "his angels," and not his "archangels." Thus it seems that there may be only one archangel.

Ironically, it must be noted that "Michael" is generally translated as "Who is like God?" This is an interrogatory sentence, and not a declarative sentence.

The Greek New Testament "Michael" is:

"*3413* Michaēl; of Heb. or. [4317]; *Michaēl*, an archangel: - Michael." [75]

The Hebrew Old Testament "Michael" is:

"4317 Miykâ'êl; from 4310 and (the pref. der. from) 3588 and 410; *who* (is) *like God?*; *Mikael*, the name of an archangel and of nine Isr.: - Michael." [76]

"4310 mîy; an interrog. pron. of persons, as 4100 is of things, *who?* (occasionally, by a peculiar idiom, of things); also (indef.) whoever; often used in oblique construction with pref. or suff..." [77]

"3588 kîy; a prim. particle [the full form of the prepositional prefix] indicating *causal* relations of all kinds..." [78]

And what about Gabriel?

Gabriel is often considered by many to also be an archangel. Gabriel appears a total of four times in the entire Bible; presented here, but not in chronological order:

When Gabriel visited Zacharias, although he states that he is Gabriel, it seems that he never identified *himself* as either an angel or an archangel.

Here in Luke 1:11 (KJV), he is characterized as an angel but only by the *author*:

> "And there appeared unto him an angel of the Lord standing on the right side of the altar of incense."[79]

And the author's characterization continues in Luke 1:13 (KJV):

> "But the angel said unto him, Fear not, Zacharias: for thy prayer is heard; and thy wife Elisabeth shall bear thee a son, and thou shalt call his name John."[80]

This characterization continues in Luke 1:18 (KJV):

> "And Zacharias said unto the angel, Whereby shall I know this? for I am an old man, and my wife well stricken in years."[81]

But in the next verse, Luke 1:19 (KJV), Gabriel somewhat characterizes himself:

> "And the angel answering said unto him, I am Gabriel, that stand in the presence of God; and am sent to speak unto thee, and to shew thee these glad tidings."[82]

Here again, Gabriel is described as an angel by the *author*, but does not characterize himself as such. But functionally he is acting as such, by acting as a *messenger* and bringing of good *tidings*.

And later in Luke 1:26-27 (KJV):

> "the angel Gabriel was sent from
> God unto a city of Galilee,
> named Nazareth, To a virgin espoused
> to a man whose name was Joseph,
> of the house of David;
> and the virgin's name was Mary."[83]

Here again, Gabriel is described as an angel only by the author. But he clearly was acting as a *messenger* and bringing of good *tidings*.

And we know that Gabe was not there to perform a miracle, as Luke 1:34-35 tells us that it was the Holy Ghost and not Gabriel who was to perform the miracle:

> "Then said Mary unto the angel, How shall
> this be, seeing I know not a man?
> And the angel answered and said unto her,
> The Holy Ghost shall come upon thee,
> and the power of the Highest shall
> overshadow thee: therefore also that
> holy thing which shall be born of thee
> shall be called the Son of God."[84]

In addition to the above New Testament citations, Gabriel also appears in the Old Testament in Daniel 8:16 (KJV):

> "And I heard a man's voice between the banks of Ulai,
> which called, and said, Gabriel, make this

man to understand the vision."[85]

The preceding verse, Daniel 8:15 (KJV), tell us Gabriel's *physical appearance* in this passage:

> *"And it came to pass, when I, even I Daniel, had seen the vision, and sought for the meaning, then, behold, there stood before me as the appearance of a man."*[86]

The actual Hebrew word translated as "appearance" is:

> "4758 mar'eh; from 7200; a *view* (the act of seeing); also an *appearance* (the thing seen), whether (real) a *shape* (espec. if handsome, *comeliness*; often plur. the *looks*), or (mental) a *vision...*"[87]

Thus it is unclear if Gabriel appeared as a physical man or "a vision." What is clear is that whether physical or an apparition, Gabriel is a "good-looker."

And Gabriel also appears in Daniel 9:21 (KJV):

> *"Yea, whiles I was speaking in prayer, even the man Gabriel, whom I had seen in the vision at the beginning, being caused to fly swiftly, touched me about the time of the evening oblation."*[88]

Here Gabriel is described as "the man." The actual Hebrew word translated as "the man" is:

"376 'îysh; contr. for 582 [or perh. rather from an unused root mean. to *be extant*]; a *man* as individual or a male person; often used as an adjunct to more definite term (and in such cases frequently not expressed in translation)..."[89]

Strong provides no original word for "being caused."

In these four passages where Gabriel appears, he is described as an angel in the New Testament by the author, but not by Gabriel himself. And in the Old Testament he is described as *"appearance of a man;"* (Daniel 8:15); and *"the man Gabriel"* (Daniel 9:21).

And Gabriel is clearly admitting that he is acting in the literal functional capacity of an *aggĕlŏs*, in that he is there to *"speak unto thee,"* and *"shew thee these glad tidings."* Functionally, Gabriel is both a messenger and one involved in bringing tidings.

But what is Gabriel *structurally*? "Gabriel" is generally understood to mean "man of God."

According to Strong, New Testament *Greek* "Gabriel" is:

"*1043* Gabriēl; of Heb. or. 1403](sic.); *Gabriel*, an archangel: - Gabriel."[90]

Here Strong is "punting" to the Hebrew, with the assumption of *archangel* status, just as many others believe. But the Hebrew Gabriel is:

"1403 Gabrîy'êl; from 1397 and 410; *man of God; Gabriel*, an archangel: - Gabriel."[91]

"1397 geber; from 1396; prop. a *valiant* man or *warrior*; gen. a *person* simply: - everyone, man, x mighty."[92]

"1396 gâbar; a prim. root; to *be strong*; by impl. to *prevail, act insolently...*"[93]

"410 'êl; short. from 352; *strength*; as adj. *mighty*; espec. the *Almighty* (but used also of any *deity*)..."[94]

"352 'ayîl; from the same as 193; prop. *strength*; hence anything *strong*; spec. a *chief* (politically); also a *ram* (from his strength); a *pilaster* (as a strong support); an *oak* or other strong tree..."[95]

"193 'ûwl; from an unused root mean. to *twist*, i.e. (by impl.) *be strong*; the *body* (as being *rolled* together); also *powerful*: - mighty, strength."[96]

Thus although *functionally*, Gabriel clearly is an *aggĕlŏs*, or angel; however *structurally*, the evidence strongly suggests that he is like a man—and a very "strong" and "valiant" man; and here again likely quite "good looking."

Why does this matter? Because; most consider the status of "angel(s)" as a *structural* phenomenon, that is or are engaging in various types of different acts. But the status of whether or not one is an *aggĕlŏs*/angel; seems to depend much more on *function*, rather than *structure*.

With regard to Michael and Gabriel, each is *aggĕlŏs* functionally, but seemingly entirely different structurally. It is not known what other different structural entities in the immaterial realm may likewise be considered *aggĕlŏs* functionally, despite a plethora of different structures.

What is "out there" with regard to the structure of "angels?

There is this "theory" that the structure of "angels" consists of nine different forms, grouped into three categories or "spheres." The first category or "sphere" is the highest rank, and consists of: Seraphim, Cheribum, and Thrones. The second is the "middle rank" and consists of Dominions, Virtues, and Powers. And the third or "lowest rank" consists of: Principalities, Archangels and Angels.[97]

As can be seen, here angels are the lowest in terms of rank, despite the fact that all are considered as "angels" in this "hierarchy." The spelling of cheribum, as opposed to cherubim is noted.

This same source cites a 5th century scholar named Dionysius as the author of this hierarchy. *This* Dionysius; "studied the references to Angels in the Scriptures and other non-biblical sources."[98] The key phrase here is "and other non-biblical sources." Firstly; it remains unclear how the Scriptures can be considered as a "non-biblical" source; which is at a minimum implied by the use of other." Secondly, these unidentified "non-biblical" sources; make the entire "theory" highly suspect.

Another source credits *another* Dionysius with authorship of this "theory." According to this source; it was: "St Dionysius who was a student of Apostle Paul," who is the author of this same theory.[99]

Paul is believed to have been born around 5 AD, and not 500 AD. Ergo, this could not be the same Dionysius as is cited by the previous source—by about four to five hundred years.

The only time the name "Dionysius" could be found in the Bible, is in Acts 17:34:

> *"Howbeit certain men clave unto him,
> and believed: among the which was Dionysius
> the Areopagite, and a woman named
> Damaris, and others with them."*[100]

And the only things we are told about *this* Dionysius, is that he "believed" Paul and "clave unto him."

The original Greek word translated as "clave" is:

> "2853 kŏllaō; from kŏlla (*"glue"*); to *glue* i.e. (pass. or reflex.) to *stick* (fig.): - cleave, join (self), keep company."[101]

Thus it is entirely possible that Dionysius merely hugged Paul; and in fact never became any type of "student." Except for believing Paul, and "*clave unto him;*" there seems to be no Biblical record of Dionysius ever doing anything else.

But two of these words purporting to be angels in various "structural" forms do warrant some analysis:

Cherubim, Cherubims, Cherub are all:

> "3742 kerûwb; of uncert. der.; a *cherub* or imaginary figure: - cherub, [*plur.*] cherubims."[102]

This is obviously not particularly helpful, unless "imaginary" here is meant to be synonymous with cherub, meaning existing only in one's reality.

As will be addressed again shortly, there is a Hebrew word translated as "sword" which is:

> "2719 chereb; from 2717 *drought*; also a *cutting* instrument (from its *destructive* effect), as a *knife, sword*, or other sharp implement.: - axe, dagger, knife, mattock, sword, tool."[103]

The first appearance of "Cherub," is in the plural as "Cherubims" in Genesis 3:24 (KJV):

> "So he drove out the man; and he placed
> at the east of the garden of Eden
> Cherubims, and a flaming sword
> which turned every way, to keep the
> way of the tree of life."[104]

So here we are told that there are "kᵉrûwb (Cherubims), and a flaming chereb (sword)." Thus as it reads, there is more than one Cherub, but only one flaming sword.

Flaming is:

"3858 lahaṭ; from 3857; a *blaze*; also (from the idea of *enwrapping*) *magic* (as *covert*): - flaming, enchantment."[105]

Thus it seems that "magic sword" would also be a fair translation.

According to Strong, Genesis 3:24 originally read as "The Cherubim;" and was later changed to read "Cherubims."[106] Strong also indicates that what now is read as "flaming," used to be "the flame of a."[107]

The Interlinear Bible translates this as: "the cherubim and the flaming sword whirling around."[108]

Ezekiel 10:15-17 (KJV) provides only slight clarity:

*"And the cherubims were lifted up.
This is the living creature that I saw by the river
of Chebar. And when the cherubims went,
the wheels went by them: and when the
cherubims lifted up their wings to mount
up from the earth, the same wheels
also turned not from beside them.
When they stood, these stood;
and when they were lifted up, these
lifted up themselves also: for the spirit of
the living creature was in them."*[109]

There are at least two entities described here in these passages. There are the "cherubims" and the "living creature." It seems fair that the "cherubims" were lifted by the "living creature." Thus it seems that the "cherubims" may have been incapable of lifting themselves, perhaps they were not any type of "being." But then we are told *"when the cherubims lifted up their wings to mount up from the earth."* Here it seems that the cherubim were "beings" of some type. Then we are told: *"When they stood, these stood; and when they were lifted up, these lifted up themselves also: for the spirit of the living creature was in them:"*—perhaps suggesting that the cherubim were inanimate, until animated by the *"spirit of the living creature.*" In fact, by distinguishing the "living creature" from these cherubim, there is a strong implication that these cherubim were not living. Whether "living" here means physically alive, or spiritually alive, or merely a "being;" remains at best unclear.

To make matters even worse, Vines states that cherubim: "...represent redeemed human beings in union with Christ, a union seen, figuratively, proceeding out of the Mercy Seat."[110]

In fact there seems little evidence to suggest that cherubim should be characterized as angels. This purported "hierarchy" is one of "angels," yet only the last two on the bottom are called angels. Simply because certain beings may (lawfully) exist in the immaterial realm, does not necessarily mean that they are angels. Unless of course one assumes that if any being in the immaterial realm is not God or a human soul; then it must necessarily then be an angel, no matter what may be its *structure* or *function*.

There are only two times that the word Seraphim(s) appears in the entire Bible. Isaiah 6:2 and Isaiah 6:6. It seems little wonder why either Dionysius the *former*, or Dionysius the *latter*, was forced to utilize "other non-biblical sources."

Isaiah 6:2 (KJV):

> "*Above it stood the seraphims: each one had six wings; with twain he covered his face, and with twain he covered his feet, and with twain he did fly.*"[111]

Isaiah 6:6 (KJV):

> "*Then flew one of the seraphims unto me, having a live coal in his hand, which he had taken with the tongs from off the altar:*"[112]

The actual Hebrew word translated as seraphims is:

"8314 sârâph; from 8313; *burning*, i.e. (fig.) *poisonous* (serpent); spec. a saraph or symbol. Creature (from their copper color): - fiery (serpent) saraph."[113]

Thus the purported angel "hierarchy," places one whose actual name means "*burning*, i.e. (fig.) *poisonous* (serpent);" right under God, and many "degrees of rank" above Michael.

This "hierarchy" is likely patent nonsense. But of course although determining one "theory" to be nonsense, sheds light on only what *is not* so; but unfortunately provides no information regarding what *is* so. The truth is; that it seems there is at best only *doxa* available.

In addition to acting as messengers or bringers of good tidings, what type of other acts are or were *aggĕlŏs* involved in?

Following are just a few examples:

In Genesis 19, angels partially blind "men:"

Genesis 19:1 (KJV) tells us:

> "And there came two angels to Sodom at even;
> and Lot sat in the gate of Sodom:
> and Lot seeing them rose up to meet them;
> and he bowed himself with his face
> toward the ground;"[114]

In Genesis 19:11 (KJV), the "they," are these same angels from the above verse 1:

> "And they smote the men that were at the door
> of the house with blindness, both small
> and great: so that they wearied themselves
> to find the door."[115]

The actual Hebrew word translated here as "blindness" is:

"5575 çanvêr; of uncert. der.; (in plur.) *blindness*: - blindness."[116]

In 1 Kings 19:5-7 (KJV), Elijah is fed by angels:

"And as he lay and slept under a juniper tree, behold, then an angel touched him, and said unto him, Arise and eat. And he looked, and, behold, there was a cake baken on the coals, and a cruse of water at his head.

And he did eat and drink, and laid him down again. And the angel of the Lord came again the second time, and touched him, and said, Arise and eat; because the journey is too great for thee."[117]

In Matt 4:11 (KJV) angels minister to Jesus:

"Then the devil leaveth him, and, behold, angels came and ministered unto him."[118]

The actual Greek word translated as "ministered" is:

"1247 diakŏnĕō; from 1249; to *be an attendant*, i.e. *wait upon* (menially or as a host, friend or [fig.] teacher); techn. *to act as a* Chr. *deacon...*"[119]

It is unclear here precisely what these "angelic attendants" actually attended to; other than this seems a bit more than merely being a messenger, or bringing tidings. It seems unlikely that Jesus had any need for a Christian deacon at that time.

Acts 12:6-10 (KJV) angels help Peter escape from prison:

> "And when Herod would have brought him
> forth, the same night Peter was sleeping between
> two soldiers, bound with two chains: and the keepers
> before the door kept the prison.
>
> And, behold, the angel of the Lord
> came upon him, and a light shined in the
> prison: and he smote Peter on the side,
> and raised him up, saying, Arise up quickly.
> And his chains fell off from his hands.
>
> And the angel said unto him, Gird thyself,
> and bind on thy sandals. And so he did.
> And he saith unto him, Cast thy garment
> about thee, and follow me.
>
> And he went out, and followed him; and wist
> not that it was true which was done by
> the angel; but thought he saw a vision.
> When they were past the first and the second
> ward, they came unto the iron gate that
> leadeth unto the city; which opened to them
> of his own accord: and they went out,
> and passed on through one street;
> and forthwith the angel departed from him."[120]

In Acts 12:23 (KJV), angels kill Herod:

> "And upon a set day Herod, arrayed in royal
> apparel, sat upon his throne, and made
> an oration unto them.
>
> "And the people gave a shout, saying,
> It is the voice of a god, and not of a man.
> And immediately the angel of the Lord
> smote him, because he gave not God the glory:
> and he was eaten of worms, and gave up the ghost."[121]

In 1 Chronicles 21:30 (KJV), angels protect an area:

> *"But David could not go before it to enquire of God: for he was afraid because of the sword of the angel of the Lord."*[122]

The actual Hebrew word translated here as "sword" is: the previously referenced:

> "2719 chereb; from 2717 *drought*; also a *cutting* instrument (from its *destructive* effect), as a *knife, sword*, or other sharp implement.: - axe, dagger, knife, mattock, sword, tool."[123]

It must be asked what a "drought" has to do with a cutting instrument? Perhaps drought refers to exsanguination by cutting. More likely, it is because of the reliance of an agricultural community upon rainfall; and thus the extreme destructive power of a drought. It must be noted that according to Strong, every translation of chereb, (the words after the : -), represents either some type of cutting instrument or a "tool."

So in addition to being a messenger, or bringer of tidings, angels also:

- Blinded, at least temporarily, a group of "men."
- Fed Elijah.
- Attended to, or "waited on" Jesus.
- Helped Peter escape from prison.
- Killed Herod, likely with worms.
- "Scared David" with their sword while protecting an area.

Thus "messenger," or a bringer of "tidings," seems a bit euphemistic to describe the capabilities of angels. Although in certain senses, each of the actions enumerated above did in fact send a message; and each still does to this very day.

And irrespective of their *number*; and irrespective of their *structure*; strictly as a matter of *function*, some *aggĕlŏs* were cast out of the immaterial realm along with Satan. This was most certainly after Genesis 1:1; and likely at some point between Genesis 1:1 and Genesis 1:2.

Ciò Che è Noto—
Una Ricapitolazione

[That Which is Known—
A Recapitulation]

So then what is it that we reasonably know?

At some point in "time," there was no *material* realm. Science tells us about the event of the creation of "The Universe" via the ""Big Bang Theory." Science is primarily concerned with the nature of the event itself, and the *physical* process, but not necessarily this being the result of the will of any "I am."

The Bible agrees with science in this in the broad sense; once it is understood that Adam's *formation* (yâtsar), is an event that is separate and distinct from the *creation* of the original hosts ('bârâ)—with the same (creation) likely occurred hundreds of thousands of years before Adam. The entire purview of the scientific study of this creation of the universe is contained in one Bible verse, described by man as Genesis 1:1: *"In the Beginning God created the heavens and the earth."*

Assuming "anything" existed, and of course something had to; there necessarily was some type of realm from which the *cause* for the *effect* known as the creation of the material universe resided or emanated from; as a yet to be created (non-existing) realm could not be the source of that which created this very same realm. And since containing matter or not containing matter is a *binary*; that realm which existed prior to the creation of matter; i.e. the *material* realm; could not have contained yet to be created matter; i.e.; an *immaterial* realm.

This Biblical "beginning," is the beginning of the material realm, and this "beginning" ends with the word "earth" at the end of Genesis 1:1.

Whatever it is that is described from the man placed period after this word "earth" onward, represents; either directly or indirectly; some part of the redemptive process of the earth. And this includes the later created tsâbâ or "hosts," created by God to aid in this redemptive process, or "kiboshing" (kâbash) of the earth.

Clearly the condition of the earth as described in Genesis 1:2, is a condition requiring significant repairs, which we are told God Himself began. And as stated, He would then later create man as the aforementioned tsâbâ to aid Him in this effort. This aid was not required because of any lack of *capability*, but rather because of lack of *authority*.

Between Genesis 1:1 and Genesis 1:2 there had been some "deceiveth" going on from the immaterial realm. This "deceiveth" is known as "planaō; from *4106*; to (prop. *cause to*) roam (from safety, truth, or virtue): - go astray, deceive, err, seduce, wander, be out of the way." This planaō was perpetrated by certain "aggĕlŏs; from aggĕllō; (prob. der. from *71*; comp. *34*) (to *bring tidings*); a *messenger*; esp. an *"angel"*; by impl. a *pastor*:- angel, messenger;" while they were in the *immaterial* realm.

Because of this planaō perpetrated by certain aggĕlŏs (including Satan), the earth became as described in Genesis 1:2—*"without form and void."* It is stipulated that those life forms that were the targets of said planaō at that time remain unstated in the Bible. But the derivation of something animate capable of being "deceiveth" is a logical necessity or requirement.

And also because of this planaō: *"there was war in heaven: Michael and his angels fought against the dragon; and the dragon fought and his angels, And prevailed not; neither was their place found any more in heaven. And the great dragon was cast out, that old serpent, called the Devil, and Satan, which deceiveth the whole world: he was cast out into the earth, and his angels were cast out with him."*

The conclusion of this event, (the war); likely represents the establishment of that which is known as hell, nether world, Hades, etc. And to get these entities into this area required an opening from where these entities were (the immaterial), to this established area. This area was established by God and thus this opening is likely controlled by Him. It is unknown at this point, whether this is a "two-way" opening. *If* the story of "Legion" represents salvation for any of these aggĕlŏs who were in this area (general area of hell), then perhaps there is; in a certain sense; some "way out."

Job 1:6-7 (KJV), tells us:

"Now there was a day when the sons of God came to present themselves before the Lord, and Satan came also among them. And the Lord said unto Satan, Whence comest thou?

"Then Satan answered the Lord, and said, From going to and fro in the earth, and from walking up and down in it."[124]

Job 2:1-2 (KJV), tells us:

"Again there was a day when the sons of God came to present themselves before the Lord, and Satan came also among them to present himself before the Lord. And the Lord said unto Satan, From whence comest thou?

> "And Satan answered the Lord, and said,
> From going to and fro in the earth, and from
> walking up and down in it."[125]

Job 2:7 (KJV), tells us:

> "So went Satan forth from the presence
> of the Lord, and smote Job with sore boils
> from the sole of his foot unto his crown."[126]

Thus it seems that under certain circumstances, there does in fact exist a "two-way" opening from the neither or nether world or hell to the immaterial realm or "heaven." The fact that this is under Gods control, and not necessarily a permanent opening; does not mean that this opening does not exist.

After the creation of man, sin by man was inevitable. The same could be said about Adam, once the knowledge of evil was brought to him. And the same rules would apply to the immaterial portion of man contaminated by sin as applied to those aggĕlŏs who sinned while in the immaterial—neither can be in the immaterial realm.

But at some point salvation would become available to all men. Thus those who were "unfortunate" enough to live physically before the availability of salvation, were sequestered in this kŏlpŏs, or Abraham's Bosom.

Demoni nella Bibbia

[Demons in the Bible]

Up until this point there is a word the usage of which has been deliberately avoided. According Strong, the actual word *"demon"* does not appear anywhere in either the Old Testament or the New Testament.

Following is the aforementioned story (not parable) of "Legion," according to Luke 8:27-30 (KJV):

*"And when he went forth to land,
there met him out of the city a certain
man, which had devils long time,
and ware no clothes, neither abode
in any house, but in the tombs. When he saw
Jesus, he cried out, and fell down before him,
and with a loud voice said,*

*"What have I to do with thee, Jesus,
thou Son of God most high?
I beseech thee, torment me not.*

*(For he had commanded the unclean
spirit to come out of the man.
For oftentimes it had caught him:
and he was kept bound with chains and
in fetters; and he brake the bands,
and was driven of the devil into the wilderness.)*

*"And Jesus asked him, saying,
What is thy name? And he said, Legion:
because many devils were entered into him.
And they besought him that he would not
command them to go out into the deep.*

*"And there was there an herd of many
swine feeding on the mountain:
and they besought him that he would
suffer them to enter into them.
And he suffered them.*

*"Then went the devils out of the man,
and entered into the swine:
and the herd ran violently down a
steep place into the lake,
and were choked."*[127]

This sounds suspiciously like demonic involvement. However the translation does not include the word demon, but rather *"which had devils long time;"* and *"unclean spirit."* It is not clear why "spirit" is in the singular.

But the actual Greek word translated here as "devils" is:

"*1140* daimŏniŏn; neut. of a der. of *1142*; a *dœmonic being*; by extens. a *deity*: - devil, God. This *daimŏniŏn* is translated in the singular or the plural; i.e.; *devil* or *devils*."[128]

"1142 daimōn; from daiō (to *distribute* fortunes); a *dæmon* or supernatural spirit (of a bad nature): - devil."[129] [Note: this œ *grapheme* is not a typographical error.]

Chambers suggests that "demon" can be traced to:

"Greek *daímōn* (genitive *daímōno*) lesser God, good or bad spirit, probably originally with the meaning of one that distributes destinies, related to *daíesthai* divide, allot (sic); see DEAL."[130]

Here it may appear that we have some *functional*, and *quasi-structural* information about these "devils." But it must again be remembered that the words which appears after the ": -" represent merely the various *translations* (opinions) appearing in the KJV.

"Devil" is generally understood to mean "slanderer."

In order for something to be considered as slander, three things are generally required:

- That which is said must be false.
- That which is said (or written if libel) must tend to diminish the reputation of another.
- That which is said must be "distributed" (or overheard) by a third party or parties.

It is one practice of "devils" to divide man from God via proffering falsehoods about God to man. By engaging in this slander against God, they are trying to be that which changes or "distributes destinies." This name "devil" is because these falsehoods are designed to "deceiveth" in furtherance of "planaō."

These "devils" in Legion seem to be better described as "demons," yet they are not translated as such. By "extension, *daimŏniŏn* means "a deity," and is translated in the KJV as both "devil" and "God." However the *root* of daimŏniŏn; (*daimōn*; from *daiō*); is translated only as "devil" in the KJV. And a "lesser god" at best seems a bit oxymoronic—depending upon one's understanding/definition of God.

It must again be remembered that "angel" as derived from the Greek *aggĕlŏs* is a *functional* description, potentially applicable to different entities. But with these various attributes of *daimŏniŏn*, *daimōn*, and *daiō*; it would seem that *structurally*; these entities are more similar to Michael, (Who is like God?); or Gabriel, (Man of God); although these are *evil* in that they seek *planaō*. And to remove them from the immaterial realm required a war.

Furthermore if it can be stipulated that spiritual life or connection with God is God's desire; then there is another similarity between "*daiesthai* divide, allot distributes destinies," and; "planaō; from 4106; to (prop. *cause to*) *roam* (from safety, truth, or virtue): - go astray, deceive, err, seduce, wander, be out of the way."

Thus although all *aggĕlŏs* seeking planaō are similar *functionally*, irrespective of their level of capability; all *aggĕlŏs* seeking planaō are not necessarily similar *structurally*. Daimŏniŏn likely are at the "upper end" in terms of their capabilities.

There is also the inclusion of "unclean spirit" contained in the story:

> The Greek word translated as "unclean" is:
>
> > "*169* akathartŏs; from *1* (as a neg. particle) and a presumed der. of *2508* (mean. *cleansed*); impure (cer., mor. [*lewd*] or spec. [*dœmonic*]): foul, unclean."[131]

According to Strong, each and every time the word "unclean" appears before the word "spirit" in the New Testament, the word is akathartŏs.[132]

Cathartic is usually considered to be a *substance* for; and *catharsis* is the *process* of; purging or cleansing. With the negation of "a;" in *akathartŏs*, there is the implication of something that needs to be or should be purged or cleansed, but has not been. Aggĕlŏs *not* seeking planaō are in the immaterial realm, and have nothing that needs to be purged.

However by the use of *akathartŏs*, there is also the implication that purging or cleansing is possible.

The Greek word translated as "spirit" is:

> "*4151* pnĕuma; from *4154*; a *current* of air, i.e. *breath* (*blast*) or a *breeze*; by anal. or fig. a *spirit*, i.e. (human) the rational *soul*, (by impl.) *vital principle*, mental *disposition*, etc., or (superhuman) an *angel*, *dœmon*, or (divine) *God*, Christ's *spirit*, the Holy *Spirit*: - ghost, life, spirit (-ual, -ually), mind. Comp. 5590."[133]

Thus it is clear that what has not been purged or cleansed is pnĕuma, which clearly represents various "conscious" immaterial phenomenon.

In verse 28 we are told: "*When he saw Jesus, he cried out, and fell down before him, and with a loud voice said, What have I to do with thee, Jesus, thou Son of God most high? I beseech thee, torment me not.*"

Here Legion (yet unnamed), recognizes Jesus as the Son of God, and asks Jesus for mercy, in that Jesus not torment him.

In verse 31, Legion; these "devils;" asked Jesus for mercy: "*And they besought him that he would not command them to go out into the deep.*"

That which is translated here as "the deep" is:

> "*12* abussŏs; from *1* (as a neg. particle) and var. of *1037*; *depthless*, i.e. (spec.) (infernal) "*abyss*": - deep, (bottomless) pit."[134]

A cursory read would tend to make one think that this "deep" was hell. But these devils/unclean spirits/demons had already been sent to hell. Thus this "deep" is likely an environment even worse than hell. This seems to establish an important rule, as will be addressed shortly.

In verse 32 Jesus is then asked if He would allow Legion to leave the man and enter into swine, which Jesus did permit ("suffered") them to do. "*And there was there an herd of many swine feeding on the mountain: and they besought him that he would suffer them to enter into them. And he suffered them."*

And then in verse 33 we are told that Legion enters the swine, and the herd stampedes into a lake and were choked. *"Then went the devils out of the man, and entered into the swine: and the herd ran violently down a steep place into the lake, and were choked."*

This is a rather odd situation. Legion recognizes and states who Jesus is, and asks Jesus for mercy. And Jesus then grants Legion this mercy, by permitting (suffered) Legion to enter these swine instead of sending Legion to the "deep." Then the swine all "choked;" presumably to death. It must be remembered that swine at that time were likewise considered "unclean."

And so it must be asked why Jesus granted Legion's request? One possible answer would be that Legion knew that *principle* which would later be memorialized in Romans 10: 13-14.

Romans 10:13-14 (KJV) tells us:

> *"For whosoever shall call upon the nameof the Lord shall be saved. How then shall they call on him in whomthey have not believed? and how shall they believe in him of whom they have not heard? and how shall they hear without a preacher?"*[135]

And it must be asked why the apparent *drowning* of the swine? Luke 11:24 (KJV) tells us:

> *"When the unclean spirit is gone out of a man, he walketh through dry places, seeking rest; and finding none, he saith, I will return unto my house whence I came out."*[136]

Since wet and dry here can reasonably be considered as a binary, we are told that when "unclean spirits" leave a man, they *"walketh through dry places, seeking rest; and finding none."* Here when these particular "unclean spirits" had "gone out of a man," they instead went into "unclean" swine. And the swine then went into a *wet* place prior to being "choked." Thus Legion was in a *wet* place when leaving the *swine*.

If "dry" here is taken literally, and associated with no "rest;" then Legion was ultimately in literally the opposite environment and perhaps found "rest." Why? Because Legion may have qualified themselves as a *"whosoever shall call upon the name of the Lord shall be saved."*

The problem; is that when this took place, Jesus had not yet completed the process of making salvation available. It was not yet "finished." Salvation was not available for anyone at that time. So if all of this were true, where could Legion have possibly gone?

Legion did not go to the "deep." Legion could not have returned to the immaterial realm, as neither could any human soul; because salvation was not yet available at that time. Legion could not be on the material realm in any "normal" way. This leaves one of the two "sections" of hell as the only possible destination(s).

If Legion went to the *general* area of hell, this is likely where "they" had already been prior to their *edoparisitosis* or *possession* of the man. In this case, avoiding the "deep" was all that the mercy provided by Jesus accomplished.

But if Legion had obtained salvation by becoming a *"whosoever shall call upon the name of the Lord;"* then the *"shall be saved"* would have been the result—assuming of course that the "who" in "whosoever" does not strictly refer to human beings.

Thus, it is at least *possible* that Legion "ended up" in the kŏlpŏs.

What else do we *reasonably* know about demons in the Bible?

When Aaron and the *charṭôm* ("magicians") got into their "creating contest," these *charṭôm* ultimately lost. And these *charṭôm* explained *why* they lost. The *charṭôm* explained that their loss was because Aaron had access to the "finger" or the power of God. This of course constitutes their own admission that these *charṭôm* did not have access to the "finger" of God.

But up to until a point, they matched what Aaron was doing. Since they admitted they did not have access to the "finger" of God, they necessarily derived their power elsewhere. They did not derive their power from that which was in *heaven*. Ergo; they derived their power from that which was *not* in heaven. Since what they did violated *natural law*, the proof of this capability being the very purpose for the exercises; said power must have resided in hell at that time.

Thus at least at that time, those entities having been cast "into the earth" were capable of violations of natural law up to a certain point. This represents the very definition of a *miracle*, irrespective of the *source* of the power.

It must be noted that in each of these displays, it seems *recourse* was utilized. Specifically; God utilized Aaron; and those entities other than God utilized these *charṭôm*. This assumes of course that these *charṭôm* were physically alive at this time, this being the clear impression with which the reader is left.

Or this could be phrased a different, and perhaps a better way: Perhaps instead it was Aaron who utilized the powers of God; and the *charṭôm* utilized the powers of that which was not of God. Hobson's choice tells us this source was: *"that old serpent, called the Devil, and Satan, which deceiveth the whole world: he was cast out into the earth, and his angels were cast out with him."* Unless of course there was somehow a third source—a proffering for which no evidence whatsoever exists.

It must be remembered that Aaron was doing what God told him to do, as per instruction through Moses. [It seems Moses was originally "offered the job," but demurred.] Likewise; these *charṭôm* were doing what pharaoh wanted them to do.

There seems to be a glaring but easily missed broad overview of this situation: God wanted Pharaoh to release His people; and Pharaoh and the *charṭôm* did not want to release them. Thus it was God's will that they be released; and *against* God's will that they remain in captivity. So God provided miraculous power or *dunamis* through Aaron. Had any angel in the immaterial (heaven but not the heavens) provided assistance to the *charṭôm*, this would have been acting against God's will, and history shows that they likely would not have remained "there" for long. And according to the story, at that time the "finger" of God had greater power than had the *charṭôm*.

Thus in terms of abilities or power, there was at that time a "*charṭôm-finger*" difference, gap, or Δ. A fair question would be whether or not this Δ has changed since the time of Aaron and Pharaoh.

Colossians 2:15 (KJV) tells us:

> "And having spoiled principalities and powers,
> he made a shew of them openly,
> triumphing over them in it."[137]

This was written by Paul, and *after* Calvary. The "he" here is Jesus.

The original Greek word translated as "spoiled" is:

> "554 apěkduŏmai; mid. from 575 and 1562; to *divest wholly* one self, or (for oneself) *despoil*: - put off, spoil."[138]

Here apěkduŏmai is defined whole divestiture or despoil. Yet one translation, (after the : -) of apěkduŏmai is *"spoil,"* while the actual definition is *"despoil."*

Most have an understanding of the meaning of "spoil," but what does "despoil" mean? According to Merriam Webster, despoil means: "to strip of belongings, possessions, or value: pillage"[139]

So Paul is telling us that Jesus stripped the "belongings, possessions, or value" and "pillage(ed)" of these "principalities and powers."

But who or what are these "principalities and powers" who were despoiled?" And are these "principalities" any different than these "powers?"

The original Greek word translated here as "principalities" is:

> "746 archē; from 756; (prop. abstr.) a *commencement*, or (coner.) *chief* (in various applications of order, time, place or rank): - beginning, corner, (at the, the) first (estate), magistrate, power, principality, principle, rule."[140]

And 756 from which 746 archē is derived is:

> "archŏmai; mid. of 757 (through the imp. of *precedence*); to *commence* (in order of time): - (rehearse from the) begin (-ning)."[141]

This *archē* appears suspiciously similar to the previously referenced: "757 archō; a prim. verb; to be *first* (in political rank or power): - reign (rule) over;" which is the Greek prefix for the English *archangel* when applied to the Greek aggĕlŏs.

Thus "principalities," appears to primarily be an issue of *authority*.

The original Greek word translated here as "powers" is:

> "1849 ĕxŏusia; from 1832 (in the sense of *ability*); *privilege*, i.e. (subj.) *force*, *capacity*, *competency*, *freedom*, or (obj.) *mastery* (concr. *magistrate*, *superhuman*, *potentate*, *token of control*), delegated influence: - authority, jurisdiction, liberty, power, right, strength."[142]

Here these "powers" are in fact *ĕxŏusia*; which is a mix of authority *and* capability.

So when we are told: *"And having spoiled principalities and powers, he made a shew of them openly, triumphing over them in it;"* it must be asked if this diminution was the actual diminution of *power*, or the diminution of *authority*.

Since *archē*, translated here as "principalities" is an issue of authority; and *ĕxŏusia*, translated here as "powers," is both authority *and* capability; the answer is that likely it was a diminution of both, but primarily an issue of the diminution of *authority*.

This apĕkdŭŏmai; *"divest wholly* one self, or (for oneself) *despoil*: - put off, spoil" of this authority; whether as in *archē*; or authority plus capability as in *ĕxŏusia*; means much more than might be readily apparent:

Earlier, Luke 10:19 (KJV) was cited:

> *"Behold, I give unto you power to tread on serpents and scorpions, and over all the power of the enemy: and nothing shall by any means hurt you."*

As previously stated, this was *before* Calvary. And as also previously stated, this was stated by Jesus to those 70 "disciples" present; and it was *these* who here represented the "you." It remains unclear as to what other person or persons could be included in the group "you." As written in the present tense (give), this seems to be a change in status "going forward." But it is actually an explanation for what these seventy disciples had experienced as per what they stated in a previous verse in Luke 10:17 (KJV):

> *"Then the seventy returned with joy, saying, "Lord, even the demons are subject to us in Your name."*[143]

The inclusion of "in Your name" in this verse is noted. Mark 9:38-40 (KJV), tells us:

> *"And John answered him, saying, Master, we saw one casting out devils in thy name, and he followeth not us: and we forbad him, because he followeth not us.*
>
> *"But Jesus said, Forbid him not: for there is no man which shall do a miracle in my name, that can lightly speak evil of me For he that is not against us is on our part."*[144]

The inclusion of *"in thy name"* and *"in my name"* in these verses is noted.

Again; this was *before* Calvary and thus before the "apĕkduŏmai; "*divest wholly* one self, or (for oneself) *despoil:* - put off, spoil" of this authority; whether as in *archē*; or authority plus capability, as in *ĕxŏusia;*"

But *after* Calvary, whatever level of *authority* these *aggĕlŏs* (angels) seeking *planaō* (deceiveth) possessed *prior* to Calvary, the same was largely destroyed. And whatever level of *capability* they had prior to Calvary was diminished and likely diminished substantially.

And since these *aggĕlŏs* seeking *planaō* had already been sent to hell, any penalty for disobedience had to be worse than hell. This penalty at a minimum was that which Legion "prayed" (successfully) that Jesus not invoke.

To state this a bit differently; it seems that there is no *actuality* that exists which includes the disobedience of man by the enemy et. al; *and* the continued existence of that same entity.

It also seems that initially or before Calvary, this authority over the enemy was for *"whomsoever"* acted *"in His name."* This was likely because Jesus' authority was absolute.

But *after* Calvary, the very authority of the enemy was trumped by Jesus' authority, was destroyed by Him. Thus the enemy has no authority with respect to man.

And this remains so—irrespective of whether *man* is aware of this at any given time or not.

The *capabilities* of the enemy were also affected; whether as a result of the loss of *authority* to utilize them; or the very *capabilities* themselves. The *former* is similar to the revocation of a driver's license. One may still drive, but if caught the penalties are much more severe than merely being unable to drive, which would remain in any event. This affects what one *would* do. But precisely how is it that one is not "caught" by God. The *latter* would be to revoke the car. This affects what one *could* do.

A similar action happened with regard to dunamis or supernatural power available to man, with the same being the subject of argument by "religious folks" for centuries.

John 14:12 (KJV) tells us:

> "Verily, verily, I say unto you,
> He that believeth on me,
> the works that I do shall he do also;
> and greater works than these shall he do;
> because I go unto my Father."[45]

This passage provokes great consternation among the religious "illuminati." Like bottles of buzzing bumblebees, they attempt to proffer that this passage simply does not mean what it clearly means, usually inserting "number of" before "works."

It is interesting that the *apĕkduŏmai* (despoiling) of the *aggĕlŏs* (angels) seeking *planaō* (deceiveth), likely happened after He *descended*; and clearly the availability of increased *dunamis* or supernatural power happened, (would not happen until), after He *ascended*.

The latter part of Colossians 2:15 should not be ignored: *"he made a shew of them openly, triumphing over them in it."*

The original Greek word translated as "shew" is:

"1165 děigmatizō; from 1164; to *exhibit*: - make a shew."[46]

And "triumphing" is:

"2358 thriambĕuō; from a prol. comp. of the base of 2360 and a der. of 680 (mean. a *noisy iambus*, sung in honor of Bacchus); to *make an acclamatory procession*, i.e. (fig.) to *conquer* or (by Hebr.) to *give victory*: - (cause) to triumph (over)."[47]

If one were to inquire as to precisely why it is that the name of Jesus is so hated by the enemies, this likely is one of the major reasons.

After *apěkduŏmai* (despoiling) these entities, Jesus then *děigmatizō* or made an exhibit or show (shew) of them; and He then *thriambĕuō* or caused "a *noisy iambus*, sung in honor of Bacchus); to *make an acclamatory procession.*"

This does not seem particularly dissimilar to what the agents of these entities had just tried to do to Jesus at Calvary. They publicly mocked Him. Thinking that somehow they could kill him; which they in fact did not do; they thought they could destroy Him and what he represented. Instead, His power became available to many, and ultimately was even "greater." And they unknowingly provided Jesus with license to despoil them.

The first question of course, would be precisely who were the intended spectators of this exhibit or show? And the second question is: where did this take place?

The "venue" was likely hell. Thus all in hell likely saw this. Did those in the *kŏlpŏs* as an area of *protection* see this happen through the *chasma* or "great gulf? It is known that the "rich man or RM" saw into this *kŏlpŏs*, and conversed with Abraham. Thus it seems reasonable that those in the *kŏlpŏs* also saw this event. Many argue that Jesus rescued those in the *kŏlpŏs* at that time, and brought them to heaven.

After the *apĕkduŏmai* or despoiling, what *means* were left to those entities? Clearly they continue to have *motive*. And as long as the universe and that which is contained in it exists, they have *opportunity*. But the "post-apĕkduŏmai" *means* is an entirely different matter.

At the time when Aaron went "blow for blow" with Pharaoh's *charţôm*, these charţôm "held their own" up to a point. They may have utilized *bârâ'*, or the bringing forth, or the true *creation* of a thing utilizing *no material thing*; as was the case with the the "heavens and the earth," and the original created hosts (mankind). They may have utilized yâtsar, or the *formation* of a thing utilizing existing *matter*, as was the case with the *formation* of Adam. Or they may have utilized some other process. But they did get seemingly "miraculous" results.

Once again it must not be forgotten that these *charţôm* were likely *material* living beings, and not aggĕlŏs in the usual *structural* sense; i.e.; immaterial beings. But Aaron was also a material living being. It is the *source* of the power that is the issue. After the *apĕkduŏmai*, it seems unlikely that any equivalent of these *charţôm* would be capable of any such acts today, as it was the source of their power that was despoiled.

The same cannot be said for a current day "Aaron." In fact, it is more than arguable that any "current day Aaron," would be capable of even greater works, at least according to Jesus. And this capability nevertheless exists as a *capability*, irrespective of any *belief in*, or *knowledge of*, the same.

There is a reason for the current "quasi-schizoid" *reality* of so called "black magic" today; and that reason is that the *actuality* of utilizing those "charţôm type" powers changed with apĕkduŏmai. If one does not understand this, then one must make a choice: One must either believe that these types of powers are and always were fictional; or alternatively that these powers were an actuality then, and remain so now. But likely, the truth is that although they did once exist, these are no longer available from these sources. This is stated with the understanding that these charţôm were working *against* God's will—the very definition of *evil*.

Often there are certain phenomena associated with "demonic" events. One such phenomenon is the purported presence of "sulfur (AKA brimstone)." To be accurate, it is likely sulfur dioxide that is claimed to be present. There are two possible explanations for this phenomenon:

One explanation would be that although hell or the "neither (nether) world" to which these immaterial entities were banished, is *immaterial* in nature; but it is not any part of the true immaterial realm. Likewise "into the earth" is *material* in nature, although not any part of the true material realm. Thus these immaterial entities may bring some "material essences" with them when they traverse the "opening" to the material realm. This could be in the form of actual matter, or merely the vibratory essences of matter, such as that which forms a significant part of homeopathy.

Another possibility is that these entities attempt to engage in bârâ'; but since this is no longer possible in any way resembling their previous capabilities, the result is similar to a "dud" firecracker—instead of it exploding, it merely fizzles.

Le Aperture Che Contano per L'uomo

[The Openings That Matter to Man]

Earlier four "openings" were addressed:
There is the opening from the *immaterial* realm to this general "unchasmed" *neither* or *nether* "world" area (hell), which is the route by which Satan & Co. were sent there—likely at the establishment of the same. This opening in this border or barrier is likely immaterial, and under God's control. Except for not having one's immaterial portion going through this same opening after "physical death," it is of little concern to man while "physically alive."

There is the opening from the *kŏlpŏs* as an area of *protection*, or "bosom;" to the *immaterial* realm. This must necessarily be a "two-way" opening, as the very purpose of the establishment of this area, was to permit exit from this "subdivision of hell" and entry into the immaterial realm upon the availability of salvation via justification at a later time. This opening is also likely immaterial, and under God's control. And except for perhaps to those never given the opportunity to accept salvation *since* the time of Jesus, it is likewise of little concern to man when "physically alive."

There is or was the opening from this *kŏlpŏs* as an area of *protection*, or "bosom;" to the *material* realm. The Biblical stories of Saul and Samuel; and Jesus with *"Elias and Moses;"* reasonably prove the existence of this opening into the material realm. This is or was likely a two-way opening, although we are not actually told what happened to Samuel after conversing with Saul, or *"Elias and Moses,"* after *"talking"* with Jesus. Each event was witnessed by others. This opening may or may not currently exist; as although it is quite likely, it is not a certainty that this *kŏlpŏs* as an area of *protection*, or "bosom" itself currently exists.

Mark 9:2-9 (KJV) provides the above referenced story, (not a parable), relating to this opening:

> *"And after six days Jesus taketh with him Peter, and James, and John, and leadeth them up into an high mountain apart by themselves: and he was transfigured before them.*
> *"And his raiment became shining, exceeding white as snow; so as no fuller on earth can white them.*
>
> *"And there appeared unto them Elias with Moses: and they were talking with Jesus. And Peter answered and said to Jesus, Master, it is good for us to be here: and let us make three tabernacles; one for thee, and one for Moses, and one for Elias. For he wist not what to say; for they were sore afraid.*
>
> *"And there was a cloud that overshadowed them: and a voice came out of the cloud, saying, This is my beloved Son: hear him.*
>
> *"And suddenly, when they had looked round about, they saw no man any more, save Jesus*

only with themselves. And as they came down from the mountain, he charged them that they should tell no man what things they had seen, till the Son of man were risen from the dead."[148]

The opening that is of major concern to man, is that previously addressed opening from this general area (hell), to the *material* realm. Once again, the same being the one that the enemy (as *nâchâsh* or hisser) managed to get to Adam & Co. in the *material gan* or guarded area, (often translated as garden) in Eden; to Jesus after His fasting; to Jesus in Gethsemane; as well as the enemy's other material "appearances."

It must be remembered precisely *what* it is that is on the "other side" (hell side) of this opening. And it must be remembered that the *reason* for that which is on the "other side" of this opening being there; as well as remember that the establishment and maintaining of this "area" or "areas;" is and was in order to prevent contamination to the *immaterial* realm.

And it must also be remembered that the reason for that which is on the "other side" of this opening being there is *functional*, and not *structural*. There may be a myriad of structurally different entities there, but all have one thing in common. They all behaved in a manner inconsistent with the will of God, which is by definition *evil*. This is as opposed to "wicked" or "bad." The Crucifixion was both "wicked" and "bad;" but it was not *evil*, in that it was consistent with God's will.

In a certain sense this neither or nether world is like a prison, in that all who are in a prison against their will; (at least by design); are there because of something they did (functional) which was against the will of the people. One difference is that unlike the case with hell, there are *structural* similarities with a prison, in that generally only H. Sapiens are present in a prison. Another difference, is that the length of time one can be *physically* imprisoned is limited, in that it cannot exceed the duration of one's *physical* life.

There are *aggĕlŏs* or "angels" present in hell; but not all aggĕlŏs are present there. It is only those particular aggĕlŏs; those who *functionally* sought *planaō*; or "to (prop. *cause to*) roam (from safety, truth, or virtue): - go astray, deceive, err, seduce, wander, be out of the way;" who are present in hell. But even if in fact Legion did obtain salvation, and thus "left" this neither world; those *aggĕlŏs* that remain engaged and engage in *planaō*, and did not gain salvation, or they would not remain there. Again with respect to Legion, the "if in fact" cannot be overemphasized.

There are those souls ("the immaterial parts of those who were once "physically alive") of H. Sapiens who chose to reject salvation in this main area of the neither world or "hell." And assuming that the *kŏlpŏs* as an area of *protection*, or "bosom;" still exists as a "subdivision" for those who were never given the opportunity to accept salvation; these are also present "somewhere" in a part or "subdivision" of this *neither* world.

This of course presents a bit of an issue with Lazarus and the "rich man." Assuming this is an actual *story* and not a parable; we are not told precisely *why* RM was where he was (in hell). There is no evidence of bad behavior on RM's part. Clearly since Abraham was still in the *kŏlpŏs* at this time, salvation was not yet available. So it must be asked why RM was in the general area of hell, and not in the *kŏlpŏs* along with Abraham and Lazarus?

The "story" tells us nothing about what RM did or did not do with regard to RM's treatment of Lazarus. But it clearly does present RM as being in an area that was separate from *kŏlpŏs*, and clearly not a place RM wanted to be.

This could easily provide fodder for those who maintain the extra-Biblical view of "works related" salvation. The argument would be that since Abe was a "good guy;" albeit a sinner; he qualified for *kŏlpŏs*. But since RM was not such a good guy, or at least not as good a guy as Abe, RM did not qualify for *kŏlpŏs*—even though we are not told anything about RM's behavior. Their likely conclusion: "Since RM went to hell, he "must've" been a bad (works) guy." And many would say (perhaps enviously), that it was his "richness" that was his sin.

This "works related" salvation viewpoint is not only *not* Biblically correct; but is more than reasonably contradicted by Jesus' own words. This viewpoint does however provide the basis for manipulation of the behaviors of others—this of course being the main reason for its existence. [See *"Statists Saving One,"* Chapter 10: *"The Pseudo-Statists"*]

Alternatively, this story may not be an actual story at all, but rather a parable. It must be remembered that "parables" usually have unnamed individuals; while "stories" contain actual names. Here we have a racemic mix; with one character named, and one character not named.

The purpose of this as a *parable*, may have been merely to illustrate the existence and nature of the *kŏlpŏs*. Perhaps this parable was provided to show a "just" God—a God who does not condemn those who were unfortunate enough to incur physical death prior to the availability of salvation. If so, then the reason or reasons *why* RM was in hell would be irrelevant to the purpose of the parable.

As previously discussed, God had instructed man to literally "put the kibosh" on the earth: *"replenish the earth, and subdue it."* And again "earth" as a translation of 'erets for that which was to be "kiboshed," is a bit limited and too specific. "776 'erets; from an unused root prob. mean to *be firm*; the *earth* (at large, or partitively a *land*): - common, country, earth, field, ground, land, x nations, way, + wilderness, world."

If "all that is firm" is stipulated as fair translation of 'erets, this then likely refers to the entire material realm. But even if this is not so stipulated, it is at a minimum "earth" that is stated. So either way, the jurisdiction over that opening from hell to earth; whether "erets means the material realm in general, or the earth in particular; belongs exclusively to that which was given this authority; i.e.; this authority belongs to man. There may be a substantial argument that this authority extends to the planet Pluto, but clearly at a minimum it applies to earth.

Thus again man has jurisdiction and control over this opening of this barrier *into our* material world, no matter what its composition—and irrespective of whether man is aware of this at any given time or not.

The authority of man over aggĕlŏs in general is a two fold phenomenon:

If the aggĕlŏs are "good" aggĕlŏs; "good" here meaning those who obey God and who *functionally* do not seek *planaō*; man has some authority, but it is limited authority. As previously stated, these (non-*planaō* seeking) aggĕlŏs will obey the will of man as long as man's will is consistent with the will of God. But there is a "supremacy clause," in that when these "wills" conflict; the will of God prevails.

But the aggĕlŏs seeking *planaō* are another matter. Planaō by definition is evil, as it is against the will of God. Even if it on the surface appears to be in furtherance of "good;" such as trying to "talk" Jesus out of going through with the Crucifixion while He was in Gethsemane, before he was "strengthened;" it is nevertheless *evil*, if against God's will.

One could easily argue that the attempted *planaō* at Gethsemane itself was not acting in a manner consistent with God's plan for man's salvation via the "Last Adam;" which was begun with the "First Adam;" i.e.; to prevent it from being "finished." Thus the proponents of this at Gethsemane were aggĕlŏs seeking *planaō*. And those who "strengthened" Jesus, were aggĕlŏs who did not seek *planaō*, and that these aggĕlŏs in fact prevailed.

Man has authority over these planaō seeking aggĕlŏs, whatever their "structure" may be. At a minimum those "disciples" of Jesus had this authority; and one did or does not have to be a contemporary of Jesus to be considered as a "disciple." And likely after *apĕkduŏmai*, this authority was extended to all children of God.

But merely for the purpose of argument, one could ask *when* it is that this authority is necessary?

Just as is the case with the "good" aggĕlŏs or angels; who *do* obey the will of man as long as it is consistent with the will of God; these planaō seeking aggĕlŏs would likely obey the will of man as long as it is *against* the will of God. But since they did or do not obey the will of God, and instead seek or sought planaō; it must be asked why then would they obey the will of man, if and when man's will is *consistent* with the will of God? The answer is that they would not—hence the need for this authority.

A comparison must be made between the initial action when aggĕlŏs engaged in planaō; and that which Legion pleaded with Jesus to not do. The initial actions when aggĕlŏs engaged in planaō, was banishment to hell, or the casting into the earth. But Legion likely had already been cast into hell. Thus what Legion pleaded with Jesus for mercy from, was not being cast into hell. What Legion feared was a fate much worse than hell. *"And they besought him that he would not command them to go out into the deep."* It is this "deep" that seems to be the power behind the authority. Again, the word translated here as "deep" is: "*12* abussŏs; from *1* (as a neg. particle) and var. of *1037*; *depthless*, i.e. (spec.) (infernal) "*abyss*": - deep, (bottomless) pit."

It is not clear from the original terminology of abussŏs what this "place" is. But what is clear, is that the "many" who comprised Legion were in grave fear of it.

As stated, man has control over the opening from hell to the material, and the opening from the *kŏlpŏs* (assuming it currently exists), to the material realm; and either way those *functional* aggĕlŏs in hell; irrespective of their *structure*; must obey the will of man, else the "deep" awaits them. This represents an explosive combination—and again this is irrespective of whether man is aware of this at any given time or not.

After *apĕkduŏmai*, the main capability of the enemy is *deception*. This is not to say that they did not always "deceiveth," as they in fact did. But perhaps except under highly unusual circumstances; e.g.; "end times;" they are not going to be successfully competing with any "present day Aarons." Having little actual power left, these planaō seeking aggĕlŏs must largely rely on the capabilities of man. And it is known that the capability of man to do "greater works" than even Jesus did currently exists—also irrespective of whether man is aware of this at any given time or not.

"Perhaps this is why Peter tells us that: "Your adversary, the devil, prowls around like a roaring lion, seeking someone to devour."[10.5] There is clearly a consideration of space (prowling around) as well as time (seeking). It is true that part of Peter's statement may be read as a simile, but that would relate to the similarities to a roaring lion, and not necessarily the devil's actions. Or, and more likely; Peter is attempting to describe a phenomenon for which no correct word exists; thus a description using the word "like" to indicate the closest similarity is intended, rather than an actual comparison.

"If it is assumed that devour means consumption of whatever is the object of the "seeking," then one might fairly ask why any animal would warn it's prey with roaring; prior to killing it for food? This would seem to substantially decrease the likelihood of success; or at a minimum, cause more effort to be required. If devour just means to destroy; to kill when it is not to be used for food; then likewise why would it make any sense to warn the prey?

"But what if Peter really meant that the prowling and roaring constitutes the first effort in his seeking; is in a sense similar to radar? In the use of radar, a signal is first sent or transmitted; and then the returned signal is examined in order to gain information; "stealth" aircraft being specifically designed to minimize this returned signal. In a likewise manner, the enemy "roars;" here actually meaning those "thoughts ideas and suggestions" humans get into their heads; often knowing not from whence they came. He then watches one's reaction in order to determine their specific potential level of "devourability." His goal being to "get our attention" as he did with "the woman," so that he can get a foothold with which to continue the process. Thus, he does not like it when it is the case where little or no signal is returned; meaning that he has been largely or completely ignored."⁴⁹

It is altering the will of man that these aggĕlŏs seeking planaō now utilize as their primary weapon. Once again, this was always a tactic, but never so much as post *apĕkduŏmai*.

The most *efficient* means by which the enemy alters the will of man, is the issue of shâmar. Shâmar is what God asked that man do with His Commandments when the same were enumerated in Exodus 20. In these passages, God the Father never requested obedience of the Commandments, and neither did Jesus later on. Each merely requested that man "keep" them.

In Exodus 20:6 (KJV) God the Father tells us:

> "And shewing mercy unto thousands
> of them that love me,
> and keep my commandments."¹⁵⁰

The Hebrew word here translated as "keep" is:

> "8104 shâmar; a prim. root; prop. to *hedge* about (as with thorns), i.e. *guard*; gen. to *protect, attend to*, etc..."¹⁵¹

In John 14:15 (KJV) Jesus tells us:

> "If ye love me, keep my commandments."¹⁵²

The Greek word here translated as "keep" is:

> "5083 tērĕō; from tĕrŏs; (a watch; perh. akin to 2334); to *guard* (from *loss* or *injury*, prop. by keeping *the eye* upon..."¹⁵³

Once the enemy can cause man to supplant what God said to shâmar, and what Jesus later said to tērĕō; with what he (the enemy) wants man to shâmar or tērĕō, "downstream" success is much more likely. If one believes that stealing is wrong, the enemy has a battle each and every time he desires that a man steal. But if this binary of "it is wrong" to steal, can be replaced by an analog of an "amount dependent" test of wrongfulness; (it is only a dollar), then any theft below that threshold is "okay." There is then no battle necessary to cause the host to steal below this amount. Then this threshold is gradually increased, until the man finds himself robbing a bank, and has no idea how it got to that point.

An even better way; is to get the man to "keep" the "principle" that although there are rules for others, an ever increasing number of rules simply do not apply to him.

These original attacks of "thoughts ideas and suggestions" took place from the immaterial realm before the enemy was cast out into the earth; and they continue to take place from those aggĕlŏs seeking planaō who are in hell. This must be true, as it seems that any aggĕlŏs seeking any type of planaō did not, and thus likely will not remain in or on the actual immaterial realm for very long.

It was previously stated that: "man has control over the opening from hell to the material, and the opening from the *kŏlpŏs* (assuming it currently exists), to the material realm; and either way those *functional* aggĕlŏs in hell; irrespective of their *structure*; must obey the will of man, else the "deep" awaits them. This again represents an explosive combination—and again this is irrespective of whether man is aware of this at any given time or not."

This means that man has the authority over the material opening from hell, and that if ordered to do so, any aggĕlŏs in hell must come through that opening from hell to the material or 'erets, whether he wants to or not; else the "deep" may await him. But of course these aggĕlŏs in hell want to leave.

Except for perhaps some who purport to be experts in this area, generally man has insufficient knowledge with regard to these matters. And the "source" of much of what man believes to be true, is often these very aggĕlŏs themselves who are in hell.

In the beginning of this work, the differences between *actuality* and *reality* were addressed:

- "That which truly *exists* is an *actuality*."
- "That which is *perceived* to exist is *reality*."
- "That which exists, exists irrespective of the existence of any reality regarding the same."
- "That which does not exist, does not exist, irrespective of the existence of any reality regarding the same—unless and until it is ultimately actualized."

The Δ or difference between man's *reality* of "a thing," and the *actuality* of the same given "thing," provides an extremely powerful weapon to the enemy.

As previously stated:

> *"That which is stated in the "fine print," provides the explanation as to why that which is stated in the "large print" is false—else "fine print" would be unnecessary."*

The reason that that which is stated in the "fine print" is in "small" or "fine" print; is to maintain a *reality* in the mind of the viewer that is consistent with the "large print;" but not consistent with the *actuality* of "the thing" *in-toto*. (tautology noted) "Fine print" is by intention difficult to read; both complicated and complex; and thus by intention, is difficult to understand. It is the inclusion of that which is in this "fine print" which keeps people from going to prison—at least that is also the intention.

Man's reality of any actuality is always less than that actuality. And since there is no choice but to act from one's reality; man is prone to judgment errors from either insufficient information; inaccurate information; or some combination of each.

And realities of material things are generally absent the fourth dimension or time. The *actuality* of a "new" car has a very short time duration. The car continues to be an actuality, but in fact undergoes dramatic changes as time goes on. And the actuality of most cars ultimately becomes scrap metal at some point in "time." Is the actuality of a car that which is perceived at any particular moment in time? Or is the actuality of a car the sum total of all of the various perceptions from the raw materials used to construct it, through scrap metal. From the *material* realm perception or reality, each of these "stages" represents different sequential realities. But from the immaterial realm perception, where there is no time or duration; it must be asked what reality would most accurately represent this actuality?

From the immaterial perspective, that which is often considered a unique isolated entity, is not, and in fact cannot be any such thing. "Doing good," is neither a separate nor a complete actuality. The immaterial imbalances caused by "doing good" must ultimately be balanced. This is often referred to as *karma*. The same can be said of "doing bad." The actuality contains both the original act as well as the "consequences" of the original act, whether "good" or "bad." Each and every act sets into motion forces which must be balanced. [It is beyond the scope of this work to discuss the corresponding immaterial Newtonian laws of $F = MA$, inertia, equal and opposite reactions; or $F_T = F_A \times F_R$; in terms of these "karmic" mechanisms. See the Monograph: *"Inevitable Balance"* for exhaustive analysis.]

When one does either "good' or "bad," generally each is *materially* perceived as a concluded act. In the case of "good," there is sometimes a hope or belief that another independent "good" act will manifest to the benefit of the active party. And in the case of "bad," there is almost always a hope or belief that another independent "bad" act will not manifest to the detriment of the active party. But immaterially, each of man's acts represents the causing of an imbalance, and thus will not be concluded until balance is achieved. Immaterially, the original action, and the reaction or consequences are not independent actualities, but parts of the *same* actuality.

Thus the "explosive combination" of man's authority over the opening from hell to the material, and man's authority over aggĕlŏs presents substantial opportunities for actions, but as previously stated, few have sufficient knowledge (sufficient reality) of theses actualities.

Man was at first created, and now is formed with the express purpose of redeeming the earth. Thus man has natural curiosity for that from which he is to redeem the earth. But of course curiosity and knowledge are not the same thing. And man is subject to deception from the enemy 24/7, even while asleep.

Although this can be applied to many "professionals," it is usually attorneys that are the target of this: There are two types of attorneys. There are those who are kind and caring, and genuinely wish to make peoples lives better; and there are parasites. The same can be said of aggĕlŏs. Those "good" angels are the former, and those in hell represent the latter; and there are reasons for this.

Those "bad" aggĕlŏs must cause a *reality* in man significantly different than that which accurately describes an *actuality*. As previously stated, it is this difference that gives them power. The purpose is to manipulate man into action based upon what man *believes* exists, while in fact acting on something entirely different. But there are rules that must be obeyed. "Fine print" is required.

Many drug commercials often state all of the dangers of the drug, while at the same time showing scenes with emotional appeal. This is an attempt at a diversion *from* what is being *said, to* what is being *seen*. Here the "warnings" are the "fine print." This is done deliberately in order to facilitate the protections of "informed consent."

The enemy utilizes the same tactic. The enemy is required to present the "fine print," but there are limited requirements for him with respect to man's actually understanding it. Similarly, manipulation via emotion; most especially pride; is how the enemy presents the "fine print," and tries to make sure man ignores it. After all, just like the drug advertisements; if for emotional gratification man chooses to believe other than the facts presented, that is his free will decision.

In the novel "*Dune*" by Frank Herbert, the main character Paul is residing with the "natives" on a desert planet where water is the ultimate commodity. Ones ownership of water is represented by "coins" which one wears on a "necklace." Paul asks a young girl to wear his "coins" for him, but does not know that in their culture this represents a proposal of marriage to the young girl. The tribe leader then steps in and advises Paul of their custom; but allows the girl to wear the coins with the understanding that no such proposal has been made.

The enemy will attempt to lure man into similar situations. Meaning; that man only understands part of the actuality, and will act upon that which he "knows." Except that the enemy will either not present the "rest," or deliberately present it in a manner most likely to be ignored.

It must again be addressed as to precisely who or what is where:

This may sound like the ultimate "no brainer," but the only entities that can traverse the opening from the *kŏlpŏs* (assuming it currently exists), to the material realm; is that which is in the *kŏlpŏs*, again assuming it currently exists. This *kŏlpŏs* was a "chasmed off" part of hell for those hosts who physically lived when salvation was unavailable; and perhaps for those who physically lived, but never had the opportunity to accept salvation. Thus only these entities that are in the *kŏlpŏs*, can traverse the opening from the *kŏlpŏs* (assuming it currently exists), to the material realm. There is no reliable information available to suggest that *structurally*, anything other than the immaterial parts (souls) of humans are or were in the *kŏlpŏs*. But then again, there is no reliable information available to suggest that *structurally*, entities dissimilar to the immaterial parts (souls) of humans are not or were not in the *kŏlpŏs*.

These souls (that immaterial part of physically living beings) were and are not in *kŏlpŏs* because they engaged in *planaō*, even if they spent their entire physical life engaging in the same. They were or are in *kŏlpŏs* because they did not obtain salvation via justification for whatever *planaō* or other evil (against God's will) actions engaged in while physically alive. And since it seems from the Lazarus/Rich man passages, that these entities in *kŏlpŏs* have first hand knowledge as to the "goings on" on the other side (the hell side) of the "chasm," it seems unlikely that they would wish to do anything that could even possibly send them there.

Thus it seems little danger to man to provide a means for these entities (those in the *kŏlpŏs*) to traverse the opening into the material realm just as Samuel did with Saul. This of course assumes that it is an *absolute certainty*, that it is in fact that which is actually in the *kŏlpŏs* that is being provided this means.

But those entities on the other side of the opening from *hell* to the material realm are another matter entirely. These "non-human" entities or aggĕlŏs are in hell either because they engaged in, *planaō* in the past, or are currently engaging in *planaō*. With respect to the former, this assumes that Legion could not; and thus did not; obtain salvation—even though the more compelling argument is that they (Legion) in fact did. With respect to the latter, these entities continue to engage in *planaō*, with man as their target.

It remains unclear as to why any man (or woman) would knowingly provide any opening from hell to the material realm.

What is it that those who claim to be "Satan worshippers" are in fact worshipping?

- An entity who is the father of falsehood.
- An entity that could not even defeat Michael, much less defeat God.
- An entity that was against His will, was banished from the immaterial realm to a nether (neither) realm.
- An entity who by design is and always was subservient to man.
- An entity who was despoiled (apĕkduŏmai), mocked, and made a show (shew) of by Jesus for all in the immaterial realm to observe.
- An entity who thus has very little power left to him; except thoughts, ideas, and suggestions.

When one worships something, one admits the authority of that thing over the worshipper—whether it be money or Satan. Thus any human who is a Satan worshipper, is admitting that their power and authority over "erets; or what is likely the *entire* material realm; is somehow eclipsed by that entity which has little power left.

This is as opposed to being able to do even greater things than that which was done by Jesus, because He went to the Father. And since despoiling Satan and the rest of his aggĕlŏs was done by Jesus before He went to the Father, this "buttus kickus" power is likely likewise available to man. So "Satan worshippers" in search of some type of "supernatural" powers, are worshipping the incessant loser; and ignoring the victor, and all the supernatural power available to them through Him.

This is also a problem, because it must be asked who is in charge when a "Satan worshipper" permits an opening from hell to the material realm? If it has already been established that Satan is "in charge," then what would be the value of the "worshipper" placing any restrictions upon the "worshipped," with regard to this opening?

In fact, this is more than oxymoronic, in that Satan requires any material opening be caused by that which has the authority over the material realm, since he is incapable of doing it himself. Without assistance, Satan is currently stuck in the nether or neither "world;" because of *planaō*, and his subsequent loss to Michael. Yet at the same time, that which has this authority; chooses to worship that which does not, and cannot even get "his own self" out.

But not all who cause or attempt to cause an opening from hell to the material realm are "Satan worshippers." There are a variety of individuals who cause or attempt to cause an opening for a variety of reasons. These "conjurers" attempt to circumscribe that which is permitted, but it must be asked what it is that is expected to be gained? After all it is unlikely that one would obtain "the truth" from any of these entities; as they are masters of the lie; including "a truth"—telling truth, but not all of it.

Most of those who engage in these activities prove one thing: The abject *failure* of "religion" to provide that which is sought. "Most" must be used as a qualifier; because there is insanity as well as ignorance. Because if the truth is known, and then to worship

Satan who has little power, instead of worshipping that which makes supernatural power (dunamis) available; and is the very one who took the power away from Satan in the first place; simply makes no sense.

As long as religions continue to proffer positions that are often at best "extra-Biblical," and likewise make no sense; sane seekers will continue to look elsewhere. And unfortunately, they can unknowingly let loose that which was banished, and banished for good reason.

And as is always the case, if one chooses to open a door, be certain to make sure it is closed when finished—lest unknown and undesired entities take advantage of this opening.

La Monografia è Completata.
Secondo il Libro del Padre, del Figlio
di Cristo e dello Spirito Santo.

[The monograph is completed.
According to The Book by The Father,
The Christ Son, and The Holy Ghost.]

Danté Camminatore

ABOUT THE MEEKRAKER SERIES

What on earth is a MeekRaker? This word can be broken down into two parts "Meek" and "Raker." Capital letters were used in order to minimize any mispronunciations such as Mee- kraker; but the "etymology" is actually the fusion of these two words.

What is meek? And who in their right mind would ever want to be meek? Courage, strength, and bravery are characteristics that are generally considered desirable; but meek? No thanks. Unfortunately, the meaning of this word has been distorted over time to include things such as timidity, or shyness; weakness, or cowardice, but this is not; or rather should not be so.

Chambers states: "meek adj. Probably before 1200 meok gentle, humble, in Ancrene Riwle; later mec (probably about 1200, in the *The Ormlum*); borrowed from a Scandanavian source (Compare Old Icelandic mjukr soft pliant gentle...."[AT-1]

These origins seem to be adjectival in nature, and describe a condition of humility or softness. Thus a meek person, by these definitions would indicate a humble or soft person. The opposite of this would then be a person who is prideful or hard.

Humble vs. prideful is an easy one. Who would want to be prideful? The Bible is replete with warnings about pride; and it was pride that started all of the messes to begin with. Pride may make one "feel good" for a short period of time, but as previously referenced; the Bible is quite clear that on that path there lies destruction.

But what does the Bible actually have to say about being a meek person? It tells us that the meek shall (*not will or might*) inherit the earth.[AT-2] It further tells us that the meek will be guided in judgment will be taught His way.[AT-3] The meek will be lifted up by the Lord, and He will cast the wicked down to the ground.[AT-4] He will save all the meek of the earth.[AT-5]

And what about the Bible's statements regarding being "hard?" "For their heart was hardened."[AT-6] "Have ye your heart yet hardened?"[AT-7] "... their eyes and hardened their heart."[AT-8] "But they and our fathers dealt proudly, and hardened their necks, and hearkened not to thy commandments, and refused to obey, neither were mindful of thy wonders that thou didst among them; but hardened their necks, and in their rebellion..."[AT-9] "Happy is the man that feareth always: But he that hardeneth his heart shall fall into mischief."[AT-10] "He that being often reproved hardeneth his neck, shall suddenly be destroyed, and that without remedy."[AT-11]

The actual word in all of these citations which is translated as hard is: "4456 poroo (a kind of stone); to *petrify*, i.e. (fig.) to *indurate* (*render stupid* or *callous*): - blind, harden."[AT-12]

With respect to hard, there is a clear Scriptural relationship between the same and disobedience; not being mindful of God performing wonders in one's life, rebellious, falling into mischief, and being destroyed without remedy. In addition, by the very definition of the original word, one who is "hard" is also stupid callous and blind. (If a physical heart were actually to turn into stone, you are just dead; so surely that definition does not apply in this context or usage.)

Thus, meek or soft; that being the opposite of hard; would tend to be obedient, be mindful of God performing wonders, not rebellious, not falling into mischief, and not destroyed. Furthermore, one would not be stupid, callous or blind.

The use of the term meek as soft, also implies teachable.

Hardhead: will not change mind. Hardhearted: will not change heart. Hard necked: junction between head and heart is hard, and will not permit mental change to be transmitted to change the heart.

If it is firmly established that the term "revelation" has the prerequisite of being *the* truth; when confronted with potential revelation; it has been the authors' experiences that hard persons; specifically those of the head, neck, and heart variety; will generally behave according to the "Three A's:"

> **A_1** is *anger*. This is the first response. This anger is not so much because there is a remote chance that they may be wrong, but rather when it is somewhat clear that they *are* wrong. This would be best illustrated as a line on a graph rising from left to right; with the level of anger represented by the vertical axis, and time represented by the horizontal axis.
>
> **A_2** is *argument*. This generally begins with emotionally (anger) driven arguments. As the arguments begin to fail, the level and usually the slope of A_1 will increase. When all possible arguments, logical, relevant or otherwise have been proffered, the original arguments will then return. This would be best illustrated as a circle under the rising anger line referenced above. Often, what is just under the skin, (which is generally the reason for the pride and subsequent anger) will pop its "head" out; revealing things previously unknown about this individual.
>
> **A_3** is *absconding*. When all of the arguments and the repetition thereof have unquestionably failed, the hard person will generally abscond; or run away. This may be represented by actual physical separation, changing the subject or in some other manner. This could be perceived as the disappearance of the anger line, but is

only subjective; as the true level of anger then becomes somewhat hidden.

Contrarily, the meek will weigh the value of any purported revelation; and then decide precisely what it is that merits their belief. Sincere questioning and even some arguments will be presented; but here not with the primary purpose of proving that they, the inquirer, is correct; but rather to understand precisely what it is that this revelation represents; knowing that if it in fact does represent revelation, then this will be to their benefit. A logical decision will then be made with respect to what constitutes the truth.

The primary basis for the actions of a "hard-head," is emotional in nature. The primary basis for the actions of the meek; although perhaps including some emotional factors; (i.e. passion), is largely intellectual.

In a sense, the purpose of a rake is to separate the soft from the hard. The Bible refers to separating the wheat from the chaff, the silver from the dross; hence the title.

The authors neither ask nor expect readers to believe everything contained herein. Meek or hard is not so much determined by what one believes; but rather by the *process* involved in making these determinations.

Bibliography

1 *King James Bible* Genesis 1:1
2 *King James Bible* Genesis 2:7
3 *King James Bible* Revelation 12:7-9 (KJV)
4 Strong, James. *Strong's Exhaustive Concordance of the Bible.* © 1890 James Strong, Madison, NJ p. 7 (Greek)
5 Strong, James. *Strong's Exhaustive Concordance of the Bible.* © 1890 James Strong, Madison, NJ p. 38 (Greek)
6 *King James Bible* Luke 20:36
7 Strong, James. *Strong's Exhaustive Concordance of the Bible.* © 1890 James Strong, Madison, NJ p. 58 (Greek)
8 *King James Bible* Revelation 12:4
9 Strong, James. *Strong's Exhaustive Concordance of the Bible.* © 1890 James Strong, Madison, NJ p. 26 (Greek)
10 https://www.merriam-webster.com/dictionary/nether ret. 11-18
11 *Chambers Dictionary of Etymology.* Copyright © 1988 The H. W. Wilson Company, New York, NY p.597
12 https://www.etymonline.com/word/hell ret, 11/18
13 *Chambers Dictionary of Etymology.* Copyright © 1988 The H. W. Wilson Company, New York, NY p.525
14 *King James Bible* Genesis 1:26-28

Bibliography

15 Strong, James. *Strong's Exhaustive Concordance of the Bible.* © 1890 James Strong, Madison, NJ p. 17 (Hebrew)
16 Strong, James. *Strong's Exhaustive Concordance of the Bible.* © 1890 James Strong, Madison, NJ p. 54 (Hebrew)
17 Strong, James. *Strong's Exhaustive Concordance of the Bible.* © 1890 James Strong, Madison, NJ p. 54 (Hebrew)
18 Strong, James. *Strong's Exhaustive Concordance of the Bible.* © 1890 James Strong, Madison, NJ p. 110 (Hebrew)
19 Strong, James. *Strong's Exhaustive Concordance of the Bible.* © 1890 James Strong, Madison, NJ p. 110 (Hebrew)
20 *King James Bible* Genesis 1:6-8
21 *King James Bible* Luke 16:19-31
22 Strong, James. *Strong's Exhaustive Concordance of the Bible.* © 1890 James Strong, Madison, NJ p. 44 (Greek)
23 Strong, James. *Strong's Exhaustive Concordance of the Bible.* © 1890 James Strong, Madison, NJ p. 7 (Greek)
24 Strong, James. *Strong's Exhaustive Concordance of the Bible.* © 1890 James Strong, Madison, NJ p. 43 (Greek)
25 *King James Bible* Acts 27: 39
26 Strong, James. *Strong's Exhaustive Concordance of the Bible.* © 1890 James Strong, Madison, NJ p. 43 (Greek)
27 *King James Bible* Luke 13:28
28 Strong, James. *Strong's Exhaustive Concordance of the Bible.* © 1890 James Strong, Madison, NJ p. 8 (Greek)
29 Strong, James. *Strong's Exhaustive Concordance of the Bible.* © 1890 James Strong, Madison, NJ p. 7 (Greek)
30 Strong, James. *Strong's Exhaustive Concordance of the Bible.* © 1890 James Strong, Madison, NJ p. 25 (Greek)
31 Strong, James. *Strong's Exhaustive Concordance of the Bible.* © 1890 James Strong, Madison, NJ p. 18 (Greek)
32 Strong, James. *Strong's Exhaustive Concordance of the Bible.* © 1890 James Strong, Madison, NJ p. 18 (Greek)
33 Strong, James. *Strong's Exhaustive Concordance of the Bible.* © 1890 James Strong, Madison, NJ p. 46 (Greek)
34 *King James Bible* 1 Peter 4:6
35 Strong, James. *Strong's Exhaustive Concordance of the Bible.* © 1890 James Strong, Madison, NJ p. 76 (Greek)

36 Strong, James. *Strong's Exhaustive Concordance of the Bible.* © 1890 James Strong, Madison, NJ p. 51 (Greek)
37 Strong, James. *Strong's Exhaustive Concordance of the Bible.* © 1890 James Strong, Madison, NJ p. 77 (Greek)
38 Strong, James. *Strong's Exhaustive Concordance of the Bible.* © 1890 James Strong, Madison, NJ p. 67 (Greek)
39 King James Bible 1 Samuel 28:11-14
40 Strong, James. *Strong's Exhaustive Concordance of the Bible.* © 1890 James Strong, Madison, NJ p. 12 (Hebrew)
41 Strong, James. *Strong's Exhaustive Concordance of the Bible.* © 1890 James Strong, Madison, NJ p. 12 (Hebrew)
42 Strong, James. *Strong's Exhaustive Concordance of the Bible.* © 1890 James Strong, Madison, NJ p. 122 (Hebrew)
43 King James Bible 1 Samuel 28:15-16
44 King James Bible Revelation 20:14
45 Strong, James. *Strong's Exhaustive Concordance of the Bible.* © 1890 James Strong, Madison, NJ p. 8 (Hebrew)
46 King James Bible Luke 10:19
47 Walker, J. Bartholomew *"Wisdom Essentials"* © 2017 Quadrakoff Publications Group, LLC Wilmington, Delaware pp. 53-57
48 King James Bible Genesis 1:1-2
49 Walker, J. Bartholomew *"MeekRaker Beginnings..."* © 2016 Quadrakoff Publications Group, LLC Wilmington, Delaware p. 6
50 Walker, J. Bartholomew *"Statists Saving One"* © 2017 Quadrakoff Publications Group, LLC Wilmington, Delaware p. 58
51 King James Bible Genesis 3:1-5
52 Walker, J. Bartholomew *"MeekRaker Beginnings..."* © 2016 Quadrakoff Publications Group, LLC Wilmington, Delaware pp. 212-213
53 King James Bible Exodus 7:11
54 Strong, James. *Strong's Exhaustive Concordance of the Bible.* © 1890 James Strong, Madison, NJ p. 39 (Hebrew)
55 Strong, James. *Strong's Exhaustive Concordance of the Bible.* © 1890 James Strong, Madison, NJ p. 58 (Hebrew)
56 Strong, James. *Strong's Exhaustive Concordance of the Bible.* © 1890 James Strong, Madison, NJ p. 43 (Hebrew)
57 King James Bible Exodus 7:12

Bibliography

58 *King James Bible* Exodus 7:22

59 Strong, James. *Strong's Exhaustive Concordance of the Bible.* © 1890 James Strong, Madison, NJ p. 59 (Hebrew)

60 *King James Bible* Exodus 8:18-19

61 Strong, James. *Strong's Exhaustive Concordance of the Bible.* © 1890 James Strong, Madison, NJ p. 16 (Hebrew)

62 Strong, James. *Strong's Exhaustive Concordance of the Bible.* © 1890 James Strong, Madison, NJ p. 12 (Hebrew)

63 Strong, James. *Strong's Exhaustive Concordance of the Bible.* © 1890 James Strong, Madison, NJ p. 66 (Hebrew)

64 Strong, James. *Strong's Exhaustive Concordance of the Bible.* © 1890 James Strong, Madison, NJ p. 66 (Hebrew)

65 Strong, James. *Strong's Exhaustive Concordance of the Bible.* © 1890 James Strong, Madison, NJ p. 66 (Hebrew)

66 Strong, James. *Strong's Exhaustive Concordance of the Bible.* © 1890 James Strong, Madison, NJ p. 12 (Hebrew)

67 Strong, James. *Strong's Exhaustive Concordance of the Bible.* © 1890 James Strong, Madison, NJ p. 119 (Hebrew)

68 Strong, James. *Strong's Exhaustive Concordance of the Bible.* © 1890 James Strong, Madison, NJ p. 7 (Hebrew)

69 Strong, James. *Strong's Exhaustive Concordance of the Bible.* © 1890 James Strong, Madison, NJ p. 7 (Hebrew)

70 Strong, James. *Strong's Exhaustive Concordance of the Bible.* © 1890 James Strong, Madison, NJ p. 8 (Hebrew)

71 *King James Bible* 1 Thessolonians 4:16

72 *King James Bible* Jude 1:9

73 Strong, James. *Strong's Exhaustive Concordance of the Bible.* © 1890 James Strong, Madison, NJ p. 16 (Greek)

74 Strong, James. *Strong's Exhaustive Concordance of the Bible.* © 1890 James Strong, Madison, NJ p. 16 (Greek)

75 Strong, James. *Strong's Exhaustive Concordance of the Bible.* © 1890 James Strong, Madison, NJ p. 48 (Greek)

76 Strong, James. *Strong's Exhaustive Concordance of the Bible.* © 1890 James Strong, Madison, NJ p. 65 (Hebrew)

77 Strong, James. *Strong's Exhaustive Concordance of the Bible.* © 1890 James Strong, Madison, NJ p. 65 (Hebrew)

78 Strong, James. *Strong's Exhaustive Concordance of the Bible.* © 1890 James Strong, Madison, NJ p. 55 (Hebrew)
79 *King James Bible* Luke 1:11
80 *King James Bible* Luke 1:13
81 *King James Bible* Luke 1:18
82 *King James Bible* Luke 1:19
83 *King James Bible* Luke 1:26-27
84 *King James Bible* Luke 1:34-35
85 *King James Bible* Daniel 8:16
86 *King James Bible* Daniel 8:15
87 Strong, James. *Strong's Exhaustive Concordance of the Bible.* © 1890 James Strong, Madison, NJ p. 72 (Hebrew)
88 *King James Bible* Daniel 9:21
89 Strong, James. *Strong's Exhaustive Concordance of the Bible.* © 1890 James Strong, Madison, NJ p. 12 (Hebrew)
90 Strong, James. *Strong's Exhaustive Concordance of the Bible.* © 1890 James Strong, Madison, NJ p. 20 (Greek)
91 Strong, James. *Strong's Exhaustive Concordance of the Bible.* © 1890 James Strong, Madison, NJ p. 25 (Hebrew)
92 Strong, James. *Strong's Exhaustive Concordance of the Bible.* © 1890 James Strong, Madison, NJ p. 25 (Hebrew)
93 Strong, James. *Strong's Exhaustive Concordance of the Bible.* © 1890 James Strong, Madison, NJ p. 25 (Hebrew)
94 Strong, James. *Strong's Exhaustive Concordance of the Bible.* © 1890 James Strong, Madison, NJ p. 12 (Hebrew)
95 Strong, James. *Strong's Exhaustive Concordance of the Bible.* © 1890 James Strong, Madison, NJ p. 11 (Hebrew)
96 Strong, James. *Strong's Exhaustive Concordance of the Bible.* © 1890 James Strong, Madison, NJ p. 9 (Hebrew)
97 https://healingdeva.com/ranks-angels/ ret. 11/18
98 https://healingdeva.com/ranks-angels/ ret. 11/18
99 https://www.hierarchystructure.com/hierarchy-of-angels/ ret. 9-18
100 *King James Bible* Acts 17:34
101 Strong, James. *Strong's Exhaustive Concordance of the Bible.* © 1890 James Strong, Madison, NJ p. 33 (Greek)

Bibliography

102 Strong, James. *Strong's Exhaustive Concordance of the Bible.* © 1890 James Strong, Madison, NJ p. 57 (Hebrew)
103 Strong, James. *Strong's Exhaustive Concordance of the Bible.* © 1890 James Strong, Madison, NJ p. 43 (Hebrew)
104 *King James Bible* Genesis 3:24
105 Strong, James. *Strong's Exhaustive Concordance of the Bible.* © 1890 James Strong, Madison, NJ p. 59 (Hebrew)
106 Strong, James. *Strong's Exhaustive Concordance of the Bible.* © 1890 James Strong, Madison, NJ p. 41 (Comparative Concordance)
107 Strong, James. *Strong's Exhaustive Concordance of the Bible.* © 1890 James Strong, Madison, NJ p. 73 (Comparative Concordance)
108 *Interlinear Bible Hebrew Greek English, 1 Volume Edition.* © 1976, 1977, 1978, 1979, 1980, 1981, 1984. Second Edition, © 1986 Jay P. Green, Sr., Hendrickson Publishers p. 3
109 *King James Bible* Ezekiel 10:15-17
110 Vine, W.E. *"Vines Expository Dictionary of Old and New Testament Words"* © 1996 W.E Vine copyright Bath England p. 177
111 *King James Bible* Isaiah 6:2
112 *King James Bible* Isaiah 6:6
113 Strong, James. *Strong's Exhaustive Concordance of the Bible.* © 1890 James Strong, Madison, NJ p. 121 (Hebrew)
114 *King James Bible* Genesis 19:1
115 *King James Bible* Genesis 19:11
116 Strong, James. *Strong's Exhaustive Concordance of the Bible.* © 1890 James Strong, Madison, NJ p. 83 (Hebrew)
117 *King James Bible* 1 Kings 19:5-7
118 *King James Bible* Matthew 4:11
119 Strong, James. *Strong's Exhaustive Concordance of the Bible.* © 1890 James Strong, Madison, NJ p. 22 (Greek)
120 *King James Bible* Acts 12:6-10
121 *King James Bible* Acts 12:23
122 *King James Bible* 1 Chronicles 21:30
123 Strong, James. *Strong's Exhaustive Concordance of the Bible.* © 1890 James Strong, Madison, NJ p. 43 (Hebrew)
124 *King James Bible* Job 1:6-7
125 *King James Bible* Job 2:1-2
126 *King James Bible* Job 2:7

127 *King James Bible* Luke 8:27-30
128 Strong, James. *Strong's Exhaustive Concordance of the Bible.* © 1890 James Strong, Madison, NJ p. 21 (Greek)
129 Strong, James. *Strong's Exhaustive Concordance of the Bible.* © 1890 James Strong, Madison, NJ p. 21 (Greek)
130 *Chambers Dictionary of Etymology.* Copyright © 1988 The H. W. Wilson Company, New York, NY p. 264
131 Strong, James. *Strong's Exhaustive Concordance of the Bible.* © 1890 James Strong, Madison, NJ p. 9 (Greek)
132 Strong, James. *Strong's Exhaustive Concordance of the Bible.* © 1890 James Strong, Madison, NJ p. 129
133 Strong, James. *Strong's Exhaustive Concordance of the Bible.* © 1890 James Strong, Madison, NJ p. 58 (Greek)
134 Strong, James. *Strong's Exhaustive Concordance of the Bible.* © 1890 James Strong, Madison, NJ p. 7 (Greek)
135 *King James Bible* Romans 10:13-14
136 *King James Bible* Luke 11:24
137 *King James Bible* Colossians 2:15
138 Strong, James. *Strong's Exhaustive Concordance of the Bible.* © 1890 James Strong, Madison, NJ p. 13 (Greek)
139 https://www.merriam-webster.com/dictionary/despoil ret. 9-18
140 Strong, James. *Strong's Exhaustive Concordance of the Bible.* © 1890 James Strong, Madison, NJ p. 16 (Greek)
141 Strong, James. *Strong's Exhaustive Concordance of the Bible.* © 1890 James Strong, Madison, NJ p. 16 (Greek)
142 Strong, James. *Strong's Exhaustive Concordance of the Bible.* © 1890 James Strong, Madison, NJ p. 30 (Greek)
143 *King James Bible* Luke 10:17
144 *King James Bible* Mark 9:38-40
145 *King James Bible* John 14:12
146 Strong, James. *Strong's Exhaustive Concordance of the Bible.* © 1890 James Strong, Madison, NJ p. 21 (Greek)
147 Strong, James. *Strong's Exhaustive Concordance of the Bible.* © 1890 James Strong, Madison, NJ p. 36 (Greek)
148 *King James Bible* Mark 9:2-9

Bibliography

149 Walker, J. Bartholomew *"MeekRaker Beginnings..."* © 2016 Quadrakoff Publications Group, LLC Wilmington, Delaware pp. 185-186
150 *King James Bible* Exodus 20:6
151 Strong, James. *Strong's Exhaustive Concordance of the Bible.* © 1890 James Strong, Madison, NJ p. 118 (Hebrew)
152 *King James Bible* John 14:15
153 Strong, James. *Strong's Exhaustive Concordance of the Bible.* © 1890 James Strong, Madison, NJ p. 71 (Greek)

Embedded References

References From *"It's Not Just a Theory"*

(21) *King James Bible,* Job 1:10
(22) Strong, James. *Strong's Exhaustive Concordance of the Bible.* © 1890 James Strong, Madison, NJ p. 113 (Hebrew)
(23) Strong, James. *Strong's Exhaustive Concordance of the Bible.* © 1890 James Strong, Madison, NJ p. 118 (Hebrew)
(24) *King James Bible,* Ephesians 6:17
(25) Strong, James. *Strong's Exhaustive Concordance of the Bible.* © 1890 James Strong, Madison, NJ p. 46 (Greek)
(26) Strong, James. *Strong's Exhaustive Concordance of the Bible.* © 1890 James Strong, Madison, NJ p. 58 (Greek)
(27) Strong, James. *Strong's Exhaustive Concordance of the Bible.* © 1890 James Strong, Madison, NJ p. 63 (Greek)
(28) *King James Bible,* Ephesians 6:17 John 1:1
(29) Strong, James. *Strong's Exhaustive Concordance of the Bible.* © 1890 James Strong, Madison, NJ p. 45 (Greek)

References From *"MeekRaker Beginnings..."*

(1.5) *Scripture4all.org* (Genesis 1:2) Online Interlinear Bible
(10.5) *New American Standard Bible*: 1995 update. 1995 (1Peter 5:8) The Lockman Foundation: Lahabra, CA
(10.17) *New American Standard Bible*: 1995 update. 1995 (Ex. 20:4) The Lockman Foundation: Lahabra, CA
(10.18) Strong, James. *Strong's Exhaustive Concordance of the Bible.* © 1890 James Strong, Madison, NJ p.124 (Hebrew)

Reference From *"Statists Saving One"*

(5.5) Walker, J. Bartholomew *"MeekRaker Beginnings..."* © 2016 Quadrakoff Publications Group, LLC Wilmington, Delaware p. 11

References From *"About the MeekRaker Series Title"*

AT1 *Chambers Dictionary of Etymology.* Copyright © 1988 The H. W. Wilson Company, New York, NY p.648
AT2 *www.kingjamesbibleonline.org* (KJV) (Matt.5:5) retrieved June 2011
AT3 *www.kingjamesbibleonline.org* (KJV) (Ps. 25:9) retrieved June 2011
AT4 *www.kingjamesbibleonline.org* (KJV) (Ps. 147:6) retrieved June 2011
AT5 *www.kingjamesbibleonline.org* (KJV) (Ps. 76:9) retrieved June 2011
AT6 *www.kingjamesbibleonline.org* (KJV) (Mark 6:52) retrieved June 2011

Bibliography

AT7 *www.kingjamesbibleonline.org* (KJV) (Mark 8:17) retrieved June 2011

AT8 *www.kingjamesbibleonline.org* (KJV) (John 12:40) retrieved June 2011

AT9 *www.kingjamesbibleonline.org* (KJV) (Neh. 9:16) retrieved June 2011

AT10 *www.kingjamesbibleonline.org* (KJV) (Prov. 28:14) retrieved June 2011

AT11 *www.kingjamesbibleonline.org* (KJV) (Prov. 29:1) retrieved June 2011

AT12 Strong, James. *Strong's Exhaustive Concordance of the Bible.* © 1890 James Strong, Madison, NJ p. 63 (Greek)

You May Also Like These Other Fine QPG Publications:

MeekRaker Beginnings...

From inside the dust jacket of *"MeekRaker Beginnings..."*

"The primary purpose of this tome, is the reconciliation of the word of God with science; and to do so in such a manner as to be rendered inarguable by any rational mind. As stated in the Preface: "One must choose between being a "man of science" or a believer," because they are generally considered to be mutually exclusive. If one agrees that words mean things, then an unbiased fair read of God's Word presents no such paradox. But one must read what God actually said, not merely what one thinks He said, what one was told He said, what one wished He said, or would rather He had said."

Statists Saving One:

The Malignant Sophistry of Rights Removal by the Far Left

"...under the umbrella of "liberals" or "liberalism;" (as used today); there are actually two separate and distinct groups:
"True *liberals* believe very much in what they promulgate. They are truly concerned with the welfare of citizens, and they believe in policies that will benefit the same—at least in their view. There are neither nefarious purposes, nor any intellectual dishonesty. Their

objective is to improve the quality of life (and longevity), for as many people as possible.

"...Conservatives and liberals can often agree on the *ends*; but vastly disagree on the *means*. Giving a hungry person a fish is kind; but to conservatives, teaching him how to fish seems to be a better long term solution. It is not that conservatives object to the temporary giving of the fish; but rather they object to *not* teaching him how to fish.

"True liberals believe in the dignity of man; and promulgate policies in furtherance of this belief.

"Statists; the other group usually and often erroneously grouped under the "liberal" umbrella; are another matter. It is because of agreements with liberal *policy* that they are usually grouped under this liberal umbrella; but their *motivations*, *purposes* and *beliefs* are entirely different—arguably antithetical—to true liberalism."

Why should *liberals* read "*Statists Saving One*?"

> To understand that many who may appear to agree with your *means*, have entirely different *ends* in sight; and that these ends are antithetical to liberalism. True liberalism and statism are entirely incompatible. And all along you thought they were your friends.

Why should *conservatives* read "*Statists Saving One*?"

> To understand the difference between liberals and statists; and end the confusion. Many liberals agree with many conservative *ends*, merely proffering a different *means* to achieve them. But statists have entirely different ends in sight—no matter whom they may appear to agree with at any given time.

Why should *statists* read "*Statists Saving One*?"

> To understand the true motivations behind statism; and decide if continued actions are wise. The masquerade

is now over. Either change now; or "pack up and go home" while you can, as it will never become any easier in any current statist's lifetime.

Wisdom Essentials—The Pentalogy

That Which is Difficult If Not Impossible to Find Anywhere Else—All In One Volume. Vol. I

But there are many other effects for which no material cause can be found. In *"Donald Trump Candidacy According to Matthew?,"* his meteoric rise and seeming inability to fail are explained according to Biblical principles. Since this is a non-political work, his success was not actually prophesied, but no other conclusion could possibly have been drawn—*and this was published long before he was even nominated.* In *"SHÂMAR TO SHARIA,"* the process of radical indoctrination is analyzed, and is shown to be a perversion of that very same thing God instructed man to do with the Commandments, and how this is not in any way limited to terrorists. *"It's Not Just A Theory"* examines the relationship between behavior and longevity according to both science and the Scriptures; and "according to both" also includes major consistencies. *"Calvary's Hidden Truths"* reveals many unknown facts about what actually occurred at that time. *"Inevitable Balance"* scientifically and Biblically explains that which is often observed but rarely understood: Why "What Goes Around Comes Around;" AKA *karma*, or the "law of compensation."

REINCARNATION —A REASONABLE INQUIRY

"*Often times it is emotion(s) and not facts that determine what it is that is believed to be 'in fact so.'*" —p.6

"*When truth and perceived practicality conflict; unfortunately it is truth that often becomes the sacrificial lamb.*" —p.91

"*He that answereth a matter before he heareth it, it is folly and shame unto him.*"

—Proverbs 18:13 (KJV)

    Some say reincarnation is a fact, and cite the Bible as the unimpeachable source regarding this matter.
    Others say reincarnation is fiction, and cite the Bible as the unimpeachable source regarding this very same matter.
    One of these groups is about to be shocked.

QPG Publications are available
wherever you buy fine books.

For a full list of QPG publications,
visit us at MeekRaker.com

www.ingramcontent.com/pod-product-compliance
Lightning Source LLC
Chambersburg PA
CBHW020140130526
44591CB00030B/155